organic

BABY AND TODDLER COOKBOOK

organic

BABY AND TODDLER COOKBOOK

Lizzie Vann

Photography by
Simon Brown

METRO BOOKS
NEW YORK

This 2008 edition published by Metro Books by
arrangement with Dorling Kindersley Limited, London.

Project Editors: Nasim Mawji, Sue Cooper

Art Editors: Toni Kay, Vicki Groombridge

Designer: Poppy Jenkins

DTP Designer: Conrad van Dyke

Deputy Art Director: Carole Ash

Production Manager: Maryann Webster

Food Stylist: Susie Theodorou
assisted by Jaqueline Malouf

Jacket Designer: Neal Cobourne

Metro Books
122 Fifth Avenue
New York, NY 10011

ISBN-13: 978-1-4351-0513-3

ISBN-10: 1-4351-0513-3

A CIP Cataloging-in-Publication record for this book is
available from the Library of Congress

*Although there is usually no need to peel organic fruit and
vegetables, they should be peeled for children under ten months of
age as their fibrous skins can be difficult to digest.*

Reproduced by Colourscan (Singapore)
Printed and bound in Singapore by Tien Wah Press

1 3 5 7 9 10 8 6 4 2

Why organic?

A child's delicate physiology
makes him especially vulnerable
to the toxic elements in food; this
chapter explains how an organic
diet can give your child a better
start in life.

What is organic?

A look at the ever-expanding
array of organic ingredients
available locally and from around
the world; the benefits of organic
farming for farmers, animals and
the environment.

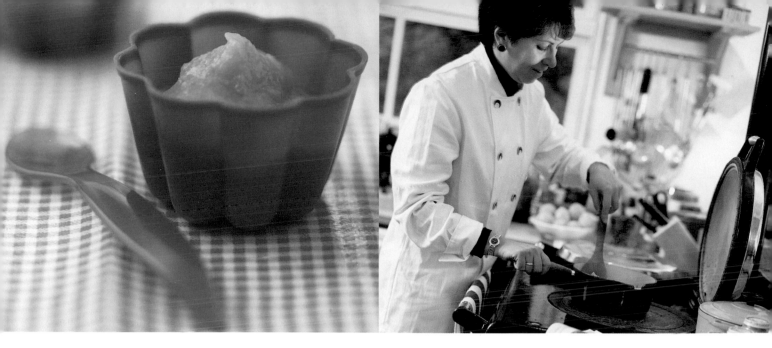

Recipes

Health issues and nutrition

Eating well during pregnancy and while breast-feeding; ensuring that your vegetarian or vegan baby has a balanced diet; advice on special diets for children with allergies or digestive problems.

Introduction

I believe that there is nothing more important than the quality of the food that we feed our children – their development, health, and happiness depend on it. This book has been created to give you lots of ideas for making mealtimes a success. It features simple, classic recipes, tested on hundreds of children.

Children like to have fun. They like new ideas, new colors, and new flavors. Many food manufacturers and cookbook writers have responded to this by disguising food with lots of bright colors and masking its real flavor with excessive sugar or salt, even arranging it into shapes such as boats or teddy bears.

Since setting up my company, Baby Organix, in 1992, my approach has been first and foremost to make sure that we have the fundamentals of good food right and that we focus on these above all else. These fundamentals are explained in more detail in the first chapters of this book, but in essence they are:

• Always use organic ingredients because they are better for your child in many ways.
• Always use natural ingredients in simple combinations – these offer the best nutrition and the best flavor.

Good food is important to children. They

• Keep sugar and processed ingredients out of your child's diet for as long as possible. The early years are critical in building a library of flavors that your child will draw upon later in life, and natural, unprocessed foods will teach children to appreciate the real taste of food. Good-quality ingredients do not need added sugar, salt, or bouillon cubes.

• Do not add artificial colorings to food – you don't need to when you can use the wonderful vivid colors of strawberries, citrus fruits, or peppers, for example. Most children love eating – the food is entertainment itself and even the fussy ones will enjoy some foods.

• Make mealtimes more fun by talking about food and sharing your time and your childrens' enjoyment. They will not need funny shapes to entertain them if they have your attention.

• Encourage an interest in where food comes from and how it is grown, because this will help children to appreciate it. Older children will enjoy getting involved in preparing food and even visiting farms and gardens.

Baby Organix receives calls from over 20,000 parents each year. Their passion for ensuring that their children eat good food comes across in the recipes they share with us, but also in their stories about visits to farms and local gardens and cooking classes that have been set up in local nursery schools.

Good food is important to children. They take pleasure in it; they need it. I hope that this book will help both you and your children to enjoy mealtimes even more.

Lissie Vann

take *pleasure* in it; they *need* it.

why ORGANIC?

Organic food not only offers your child

the very best start in life – it also offers

a better future for the world in which

your child will grow.

The best *for* your baby

Nothing is more important for your baby than safe, healthy food. All children deserve the best possible nourishment, and to be protected from harmful elements that may damage them.

HOW A CHILD'S BODY DEVELOPS

The most rapid growth periods are in the uterus, during infancy, and at puberty:

• A baby grows about 20in (50cm) in his first year and by 2 years old has reached half of his adult height; at puberty he has a growth spurt of 5in (12cm) per year

• At birth, 14% of a baby's body weight is fat; by 6 months this rises to 25%; a 2-year-old weighs 20% of his adult weight; an 11-year-old is half of his adult weight.

Hardly a week passes without another food scare hitting the headlines. Concerns about genetically modified (GM) foods, bovine spongiform encephalopathy (BSE), and pesticides are just some of the major issues that have caused anxious parents to search for safer, more wholesome food for their children.

Existing regulations are based on "acceptable" levels for adult consumption and may not protect children from toxins. Babies and young children are at greater risk because the immaturity of their organs and body systems makes them more vulnerable to toxins. Children also receive higher exposure to pesticides from the limited types of foods they eat.

The only way to avoid these threats to your child's health is to ensure that everything he eats and drinks is organic, pesticide- and additive-free, and grown in conditions that are regulated and monitored. More and more parents are deciding that there should be no compromise on what they feed their babies.

Why children are vulnerable

From conception until one year of age children are at their most vulnerable. During this critical stage of development cells are multiplying at their peak, yet the body has a limited diet to draw upon. In addition, immature organs and body systems respond differently to food: a baby's digestive system is more efficient than that of an adult at absorbing foods, enabling nutrients to be used more quickly but making the baby more vulnerable to toxins. Also, immature kidneys are not as proficient at excreting harmful substances, so they may circulate in the body for longer. Research cannot be relied upon since processed foods and chemicals are tested on adults, and scaling down the results for infants won't necessarily give an accurate answer. Also, babies eat far more per pound of body weight than adults and their fluid intake is far higher.

Pesticides are a cause for concern, particularly since research has revealed their presence in breast milk, a baby's first food. They have been found to bind to fat and once absorbed may stay in the body for a lifetime, some emerging in milk during breast-feeding. Despite this, all experts still recommend breast-feeding as best. Breast milk is the ultimate superfood, produced to satisfy your baby's specific needs.

THE RISK TO CHILDREN

A child's body composition makes him vulnerable because:

• Vital organs develop throughout childhood; a child's immature kidneys are less able to filter out harmful substances and cannot break down some toxins

• The nervous system grows rapidly in the first year and continues until the age of 18; its development can be disrupted by exposure to toxins

• Until the age of 6, a child's body is made up of more water and less fat than that of an adult; fats, which in an adult "trap" and store pesticide residues, are less able to do this job, leaving them to circulate in the body; water-soluble pesticides are also more able to circulate in a child's body.

Protect your children's health by ensuring that everything they eat and drink is organic and free from artificial additives.

Pesticide residues

For the first four to six months, babies are dependent upon breast or formula milk for their nourishment. Recent research, carried out by a team from Leeds University in the UK, revealed that over 350 chemicals accumulate in women's body fat and can be passed on to breast-fed babies. Despite this, breast milk is still recognized as the ideal baby food, superior to infant formula, which is cow's milk modified to approximate the nutritional profile of breast milk.

Babies' first foods are usually starchy and easy to purée since they are intended to smooth the transition between fluids and solids. Fruit and vegetables figure highly in the diet and unless these come from certified organic sources, they often harbor traces of pesticide residues. A 1998 survey by the British Ministry of Agriculture, Fisheries and Foods (MAFF) found small levels of residues in 10 percent of a sample of baby foods on sale in the UK and higher levels of residues in many of the common fruit and vegetables used to make baby food at home.

American studies into pesticide residues in the diets of infants and children were carried out by the National Research Council in 1993. They concluded that because these groups ate far more of a smaller variety of certain foods, especially fruit juices and puréed fresh fruit and vegetables, they were at greater risk than adults from the effects of pesticides.

Growing awareness of food quality is already changing eating habits. In 1999, over 30 percent of the population regularly bought some organic fruits or vegetables, and more than 1 in 3 parents reported giving their baby some organic baby food.

Additives

Many processed foods – hot dogs, burgers, candies, and drinks such as cola, for example – contain an alarming number of additives in the form of chemical preservatives, antioxidants, stabilizers, thickeners, flavor enhancers, and colorings. It is estimated that consumers may ingest up to 60 additives from just one convenience meal. Over 50 of the additives

Many *additives* have been found to cause or

looked at had to some degree been linked to health problems in some people, including allergic asthma, eczema, birth deformities, and cancer. Such additives can be approved for use in parts of Europe because the research has not been proven in each member state of the European Community.

There is evidence that certain additives are unsuitable for some sensitive people, and many additives have been found to cause or aggravate allergic reactions and contribute to hyperactivity in children. Many of them are banned in baby and toddler foods, certainly in organic products, but they may be present in family foods that you might feed to your child.

Genetic Modification

Genetically modified (GM) organisms are another major concern for parents wishing to protect their children. Scientists are now able to transfer genes between organisms, thus changing the characteristics of the host organism. Genes from soil bacteria have been inserted into soy beans to make them resistant to herbicides, genes from fish have been inserted into tomatoes to prolong shelf life and genes from bacteria have been inserted into corn to kill pests, which may damage the butterfly population. Many people feel that there has been insufficient research into the long-term effects of genetic modification – on wildlife and on humans. Because the technology requires the use of antibiotic-resistant genes, there is concern that their ingestion will increase antibiotic resistance in people.

In the same way that the special physiology of babies makes them more vulnerable to pesticide residues, we suspect that GM foods may have a greater impact on children compared to adults. The only way to protect yourself and your baby is to eat organic.

Baby foods are covered by special legislation. Preservatives, colorings, and added salt are forbidden because babies cannot process them. However baby food may contain other ingredients that can be a cause for concern. Check the label for the following:

• Sugars, including sucrose, dextrose, glucose, fructose, lactose, maltose, and honey or fruit syrups; use of these sweeteners can indicate that not enough higher quality ingredients such as fruit are present

• Meat or vegetable extracts, hydrolyzed vegetable protein, or yeast in savory foods, which could indicate overprocessing

• Flavorings; these are unnecessary in baby foods and introduce your child to artificial tastes

• Processing aids such as emulsifiers and demineralized whey; all organic baby foods are produced without these ingredients

• Processed starches, including modified cornstarch, maltodextrin, rice starch, and wheat starch; these often accompany the over-use of water; they are low-nutrient fillers that dull the flavor of food and take up the space of more nutritious ingredients.

aggravate *allergic reactions* in children

**ENCOURAGING AN
INTEREST IN FOOD**

Teach your child to enjoy good
food made with fresh, organic
ingredients. The following tips
can help to encourage healthy
eating habits for life:

• Involve your child in the
preparation and cooking of
meals – cooking builds a sense
of pride in achievement and
even young children can stir
raisins into a cake; the kitchen
and your child will probably
get messy, but both can be
cleaned up

• Encourage your child to
experiment with recipes and
different ingredients as he gets
older and grows in confidence;
the results will help him to
learn more about nutrition,
taste, smell, and texture

• Buy a juicer and experiment
with different fruit and vegetable
combinations; encourage your
child to invent his own favorite
juice recipes.

The benefits of organic for your child

Every parent wants his or her child to have the best possible start in life.
Parents instinctively know that an infant is vulnerable in ways that older
children and adults are not. Surveys have shown that young children eat
a lot more unrefined food, pound for pound, than adults. The types and
purity of the food they eat can have a bigger impact upon them than on
adults. As children's bodies grow and develop – the reproductive system,
for example, develops until the age of 20 – they are more susceptible to
the quality of their environment, including their food.

Organic food is grown without artificial pesticides. Unnecessary
farming and processing chemicals are not used. There are careful rules
about the way ingredients can be processed and additives such as
flavorings and colorings are not allowed. In organic food production,
strict standards will have been followed and monitored. Animals will not
have been given hormones or antibiotics, which means that you will
never find residues of these in the meat, a concern for some as there
have been fears that years of consumption of low levels of antibiotics
can have a detrimental effect on the immune system.

Many health problems in young children have been linked to a poorly
functioning immune system. Although the causes of this are not clear,
feeding babies organic food will not contribute to this problem, but will
help to build a strong immune system and make children more resistant
to disease. An organic diet sows the seeds of good health, which can be
nurtured throughout your child's life, influencing his or her food choices
and preferences. Eating organic food also safeguards your child's fertility,
enabling him or her to pass on good health to the next generation.

The benefits of organic for all the family

Although reasons for buying organic vary, health is probably top of
the list. There is now substantial evidence that residues left in food by
artificial pesticides and other chemicals can be harmful. Although the
reasons why are unclear, a Danish study showed that sperm counts in

Unnecessary farming and processing *chemicals*

Feeding babies organic food will help to build a strong immune system and make children more resistant to disease.

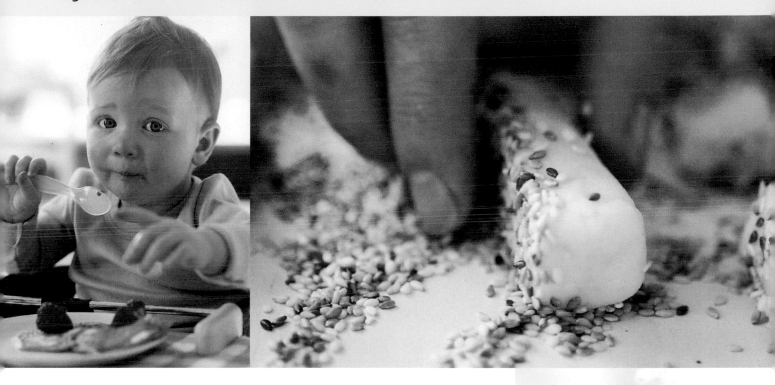

Western men have dropped dramatically over the past 50 years. In contrast, a 1994 article in *The Lancet* reported that organic farmers and growers who ate organic produce had sperm counts that were nearly 50 percent higher than men working in other professions who did not.

It is difficult to prove that organic food has higher nutritional values than conventional food, but produce does contain fewer nitrates and pesticides, less water, and can have higher vitamin C and mineral levels. Many people believe that organic food tastes better. So many processed foods contain artificial flavorings or processing aids to make them "smoother" or "spreadable" that it is becoming difficult to define the real taste of food. Eating organically is also healthier on the basis that you are avoiding hydrogenated fat, artificial additives, and artificial preservatives. I am convinced that since we began to eat organic my family and I have enjoyed better health and a greater zest for life.

GROW YOUR OWN

You can grow your own fruit and vegetables in anything from a plant pot to a fully fledged organic vegetable garden. Even the smallest members of the family will enjoy planting seeds and watching them grow. Try the following:

• Bean sprouts, seeds, and peas indoors on windowsills; they are highly nutritious and add a wonderful crunch to lunch box sandwiches and salads

• Grow herbs at home (see page 64); children are fascinated by the smell released when they rub the leaves of fragrant herbs such as basil or sage.

are not used in organic food

WHERE TO BUY ORGANIC PRODUCTS

The more you request and buy organic fruit and vegetables and other products, the more easily available they will become. Currently:

• Most large supermarkets stock some organic products

• Some organic supermarkets sell organic cosmetics, pet food, environmentally-friendly household cleaners, clothes, and books promoting an organic lifestyle, as well as the widest range of organic foods

• Farm shops and farmer's markets are a good source of fresh fruit and vegetables if you live nearby

• Organic boxed food plans and mail order companies can deliver the best produce to your door; boxed food plans are usually operated by the grower, or a group of farmers who pool their crops and send out boxes of freshly harvested seasonal fruit and vegetables

• Many companies now market their produce on the internet.

It's a family affair

Making sweeping changes can be unpopular and might harden cynical attitudes held by other members of the family. Start introducing organic foods gradually so that the family has time to accept and appreciate the differences. Discuss the benefits of organic food at mealtimes and listen to what is important to other members of your family when they talk about the foods they like to eat. You might need to be patient where their favorite convenience foods are concerned or clever in finding acceptable alternatives. But there are an increasing number of organic foods that can give you both peace of mind and peace at the dinner table. Organic pizza, for instance, is now available both in some stores and in some restaurant chains. And there is a growing range of canned organic foods such as tomatoes and baked beans, which are hugely popular here in the US.

A good place to begin your conversion program is with foods you eat often or have particular concerns about (see pages 18–19). Organic bread, milk, cheese, carrots, and potatoes can be found in most large supermarkets. Look at what is available when you go shopping. You might need to seek out the "organic aisle" since supermarkets often put all their organic produce together rather than with food of the same type. Over the next few years we should begin to see many more organic foods taking their place in the "normal" shelves alongside conventional foods.

Try to bring home something new every week, perhaps something for the pantry such as baking products, dried fruit, nuts, herbs, spices, pasta, or rice. Organic treats such as chocolate, cakes, cookies, and ice cream might help to soften the sceptics, but you could try to use the change in your family's diet to enforce the principles of healthy eating as well as substituting organic for conventional foods.

Why not make sure that there are plenty of organic yogurts in the refrigerator and a fruit bowl brimming over with luscious organic fruits? You could also use this opportunity to start introducing some more unusual fruits and vegetables.

With *organic* ingredients you know that what

Organics on a budget

When we do have to pay more for organic food, it is for the simple reason that it has cost more to produce (see page 24). Many would argue that that little extra is a small price to pay for quality and peace of mind, and in fact, prices are dropping all the time as more consumers demand organic products. Try some of the following money-saving tips for reducing any expense involved in going organic:

• Identify five foods that make regular appearances on your shopping list and try to find affordable organic alternatives

• Look out for the organic supermarket's own brand items which are often cheaper than nonorganic products

• Replace conventional lettuce (notorious for high pesticide residues) with organic white and red cabbage in salads; children often prefer its crunchier texture

• Buy organic fruit and vegetables when in season (see pages 138–39); make the most of summer fruits and winter root crops

• Take advantage of special offers; buy in bulk and freeze what you cannot use

• Check out the frozen foods aisle in your supermarket; frozen vegetables are often more nutritious and frozen organic vegetables are cheaper than their fresh counterparts

• Grow your own organic herbs

• Use your organic fruit and vegetable waste on your organic compost pile.

ORGANIC CERTIFICATION ABROAD

Several inspection bodies have been approved by the UK Register of Organic Food Standards to ensure that British farms wishing to market organic products are thoroughly inspected and maintain the high standards required.

Certification enables farms to label produce with a symbol of certification. This guarantees that a farmer has followed an approved organic production and processing system that has been verified by a team of independent inspectors.

In the UK, over 80% of organic foods are certified by the Soil Association.

you get is a *real taste*

CHOOSE ORGANIC

Tests conducted on imported nonorganic fruit and vegetables for residues of toxic pesticides reveal high levels in the fruit we eat everyday. Excluding these fruit and vegetables from your baby or child's diet is one way to reduce his exposure to pesticides, but a far better approach is to choose organic fruit and vegetables wherever possible. The following list shows the percentage of samples tested where pesticide residues were detected in 1997 and 1998:

- Oranges 100%

- Pears 96%

- Lettuce 84%

- Celery 80.5%

- Strawberries 77%

- Grapes 75%

- Carrots 70%

- Apples 69%

- Raspberries 66%

- Peaches 50%

A guide to organic ingredients

Uniformity of size and shape is not the best way to judge any food. Rely more on smell, flavor, and freshness. Even the best organic produce may not be blemish-free and the occasional insect may be found in the leaves. These imperfections should be celebrated because they indicate a lack of artificial fertilizers, pesticides, and other chemical intervention in your food. Here are some of the most important organic products to buy:

Fruit and vegetables Of all the food groups, fruit and vegetables have the highest pesticide residues, and buying organic is the best way to avoid them. Seasonal, naturally grown and harvested produce is more flavorsome. Look into organic boxed food plans: they deliver seasonal fresh fruit and vegetables to your door.

Milk and dairy products These are some of the biggest organic sellers in supermarkets. Organic milk differs from the conventional quart because the cows feed on organic pastures, hay, and silage, have freedom to roam, and do not suffer the indignities of prophylactic drugs and other treatments designed to maximize their yields to unacceptable levels. Organic dairies tend to be smaller concerns; the milk and other dairy products they produce have a purity that can be relied upon, and a noticeably sweeter, cleaner flavor.

Meat and poultry Organically farmed varieties are now widely available, offering more humanely produced alternatives to conventionally force-fed creatures that are routinely injected with growth hormones and antibiotics. Scares such as BSE have prompted public questioning and a wave of abhorrence against farming methods that include unnatural foodstuffs for animals. Organic farms operate strict regulations and consider the welfare of their stock as well as production. A better life for stock, humane slaughtering, and good butchering techniques give an organic end product better flavor. Often with lower water contents, organic meats also shrink less during cooking so they go further and have a better texture. Both chickens reared for meat and for egg production live a more natural life, unlike their caged cousins.

Fish Much of the fish available today has been reared in fish farms. This means that they will have been caged underwater, fed an unnatural diet, and treated with pesticides to prevent the spread of disease. Organic fish – especially salmon and trout – is increasingly available. The fish are reared in high-quality water, fed the same diet that they would eat in the wild, and are not subjected to pesticides or artificial treatments.

Bread and flour Cereal crops are regularly sprayed with pesticides that collect in the grain's outer layers, raising concerns about residues in bread, cakes, and cookies. The lack of artificial additives in an organic loaf, from dough conditioners to chemical improvers, gives the bread a more wholesome flavor and texture. There is also a wide range of organic pasta available.

Oils and butter Organic vegetable oils are produced from organic crops and are pressed, not solvent-extracted, a process that can introduce toxic molecules. The increasing risk of genetically modified (GM) products being used in oils is one very good reason to seek out organic labels, all of which exclude GM ingredients. In 1996 butter samples were tested and half contained traces of lindane, a proven carcinogen.

COOKING ORGANIC FRUIT AND VEGETABLES

There is no better way to enjoy the full nutritional value of organic fruit and vegetables than to eat them raw. Where cooking is preferred, you may even find that your favorite recipes taste better. Try the following tips:

• Reduce the cooking time; food loses its nutrients from the time it is harvested, but this loss speeds up during cooking, and high temperatures accelerate the process

• Lightly steam or stir-fry vegetables – they will taste and look better than boiled ones

• Use a blender to make healthy purées, soups, and sauces

• Find out about organic cooking courses.

There is no better way to enjoy the full nutritional value of organic fruit and vegetables than to eat them raw

As nature
intended

ORGANIC FARM VISITS

A visit to an organic farm provides a good opportunity to learn about where food comes from and how it is produced. It can also be an enjoyable day out. There are organizations that can put you in touch with organic farms that are open to the public. Children might like to do some of the following on a farm visit:

• Watch how cows are milked and feel the suction of a milking machine on their fingers

• Learn about what the different animals eat and help feed them

• See how various crops grow and help to pick or harvest them

• Enjoy a picnic in the countryside – you may be able to buy some of your food from the farm store.

Farms that are open to the public should have hand-washing facilities; always make sure that children wash their hands before leaving the farm.

Organic farming relies on the principle of sustainability. To ensure that our resources are there for the next generation, whatever is taken from the soil must be returned and its health must be looked after.

Farmers build fertility into the soil using animal manures, remains of spent crops, and natural rock and vegetable extracts. They rotate crops to avoid exhausting the soil and outwit weeds using mechanical means rather than sprays. The use of artificial fertilizers and pesticides is forbidden, and natural predators are used to control disease. It takes at least two years for a conventional farm to build natural fertility, allow pesticide residues to diminish, and become recognized as organic.

The benefits of organic for farmers

More farm workers are needed on organic farms than on conventional farms as more tasks are carried out manually than by machine, and animals are cared for by stockmen and women who have regular contact with them. This human link helps to retain jobs in the countryside, keeping together small communities, and it also helps us to stay in touch with a fundamental part of our lives – that of food production.

Farmers who farm conventionally using artificial chemicals (many of which were developed from chemical warfare in the Second World

Animals on organic farms are fed with a varied, often organic diet – they are not fed animal products, drugs, or antibiotics.

War), may be putting themselves at risk simply because so little is known about the long-term effects they can have on the environment, people, and animals. Despite protestations from chemical companies about the safety of their products if used correctly, the instructions are often hard or impossible to follow in the field.

Caring for animals

In conventional agriculture animals are too often treated as components in the food chain. They may be reared in cramped conditions that are

ORGANIC FARMING PRACTICE

While they expect to produce the optimum harvest, organic farmers follow the techniques of traditional farmers. They aim to:

• Preserve the countryside, not pollute it

• Recycle rather than deplete resources

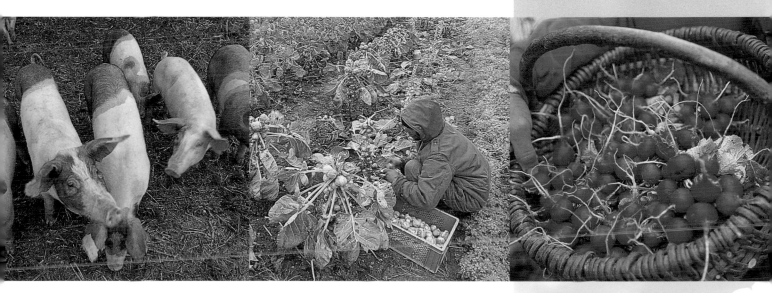

not compatible with their physiology and instinctive behavior, and as a result are more prone to disease. To combat this, they may be routinely given antibiotics – a practice causing concern among doctors who fear this may contribute to the growth in antibiotic resistance among humans. On organic farms, herbal and homeopathic treatments are used and it is only if the animal fails to respond to these that it is withdrawn from the organic system and treated conventionally. Livestock is kept in far kinder conditions on organic farms, where freedom to roam is a high priority. Free-range access to pasture and good housing reduces stress levels, thereby strengthening an animal's natural immunity and reducing susceptibility to disease. Animals are well looked after and fed with a varied, often organic diet, not fed animal products, drugs, or antibiotics.

• Build fertility in the soil through crop rotation rather than by adding synthetic nitrogenous fertilizers

• Control pests with mechanical means and natural predators rather than by using chemical pesticides

• Protect wildlife living on their land in order to encourage biological diversity.

A food system that destroys wildlife ignores the ecosystem and the way that life works.

ORGANIC CERTIFICATION AROUND THE WORLD

If a food has been produced outside the US, in order to be certified organic in the US the standards used have to be inspected and approved by one of the US certifcation bodies.

Worldwide bodies such as the International Federation of Organic Agricultural Movements (IFOAM) exist to:

• Promote and improve organic food and farming standards

• Make sure that what is organic in one country meets the standards of organic inspection in another.

Where our food comes from

More and more, the organic food you eat comes from local organic farms. Still, much of the organic produce you buy is shipped to your organic market from around the country, and some is imported into the US from around the world. When you choose organic food you are supporting small farmers all over the world.

Milk You should choose your milk carefully, for your own sake and for that of your child. The purity (or impurity) of the milk that you drink can be transferred to your child in your breast milk, so to protect your child it is important to drink organic milk yourself. Traces of lindane, a pesticide that has been linked with cancer if consumed over a long period of time, have been found in conventional milk. Organic milk is now available in many supermarkets. A large number of organic dairy products on sale in the US are produced here and include a wide range of yogurts, cheeses, cream, and ice cream.

Apples One of the most difficult fruits to grow organically because of the range of pests and diseases that can affect them, apples are grown successfully in the US, Italy, Australia, and the UK. Organic farmers grow disease-resistant varieties and introduce natural predators such as ladybugs to deal with pests. They do not wax the fruit in the way that conventional producers do; the shiny, blemish-free apple may look the best, but it could have harmful insecticide, fungicide, or herbicide residues sealed into it. Some of these pesticides wash off in the rain, but others are sealed in with wax and can be removed only by peeling.

Oranges Pesticide residues were found in every supermarket- and store-bought orange during government tests in the UK in 1999 – 68 percent contained three or more chemicals, 40 percent four or more, and many had five or six. Search out organic oranges and juice from California and imports from Spain, Portugal, and Israel. You can also find organic orange juice made from organic orange juice concentrate.

Bananas One of the most popular fruits in the US and a common weaning food, bananas are the fifth most important food commodity worldwide. Look for organic bananas from Brazil. They are planted far enough apart to prevent the spread of disease and grown with plants such as acacia trees, which fix nitrogen and naturally fertilize the soil. In contrast, Costa Rica, a leading banana producer and exporter, is the world's largest user of agrochemicals per head of population.

Rice In China, rice changed from being extensively farmed to intensively farmed in the 1960s with the introduction of synthetic fertilizers. Years later, farmers are concerned that the land is getting more compacted and more difficult to work and blame it on the use of artificial chemicals. They say that the rice is harder and does not taste as good. Rice, along with wheat, is one of the most heavily sprayed crops, so it is worth looking for organic brands in order to safeguard your child from the residues that may be present in nonorganic varieties.

JUSTIFYING THE EXPENSE

When organic food costs more (and this is not always the case), higher prices reflect the care taken in its production:

• Yields are lower because they are not artificially enhanced using growth hormones and synthetic fertilizers

• Animals are reared in humane conditions with care taken to respect their welfare; this means that both land and labor costs are higher than in conventional farming

• Organic farmers and food companies are usually smaller than their conventional counterparts; they produce in smaller quantities and as a result have none of the financial advantages of bulk buying or economies of scale

• The testing regimes to ensure that foods are pesticide- and GM-free can be a financial burden for organic food companies.

Organics around the world

Sustainable and organic foods are grown for two reasons – either because they are part of a natural farming system that has been in use for centuries; or because public concern has pressured farmers into adopting a more natural system of farming where they had previously practiced an industrial style of agriculture. Generally the food is produced by reassuringly small concerns where attention to detail is a way of life. Sustainable, organic farming is practiced all over the world and is well established in many countries.

The US is the largest producer of organic food with sales worth over $2.8 billion a year, driven by government concerns about artificial pesticides and a directive to label conventionally produced foods with the pesticides used in their production – a move fiercely resisted by the agrochemical industry. We can expect to see more organic farms like Fairview Gardens in southern California, which has 12 acres of land and is surrounded by a city. The land has been carefully nurtured into producing a variety of organic crops. In a good year, they harvest over 30,000lb (13,500kg) of peaches, plums, and citrus fruit, and tons of fresh vegetables, avocados, berries, and herbs for the local population.

Worldwide the organic movement is growing and expanding. Having adopted an organic agriculture policy in 1990, Cuba took just six years to become self-sufficient in basic fruit and vegetables. The use of artificial pesticides and nitrate fertilizers has been dramatically reduced and biological means are used to control around 80 percent of pests. In Peru, terraces cut into the steep slopes of the Andes are still producing crops of organic beans and barley for Peruvian farmers today, as they did for their Inca ancestors.

Europe is a special case. There, organic farming varies widely. In Italy there are some 30,000 organic farms, producing everything from olives to oranges. Small farmers' cooperatives, whose products include organic pasta, olive oil, vinegar, and wines, were set up around 30 years ago. Sweden, which in 2000 has cut artificial pesticide use to 25 percent

Organic farming is practiced *worldwide* and

of what it was in 1987 and has banned 37 artificial pesticides because of the damage they cause to health or the environment, has 3,400 organic farms. In Germany, the baby food industry is largely organic.

In recent years organic land in the UK has risen from less than one percent to more than two percent – while this is a large increase, it is still woefully behind other countries around the world and especially the rest of Europe where the acreage of organic land has been rising by an average of 25 percent a year. In Austria, for example, there are over 20,000 organic farmers whereas in the UK there are 1,500.

In other parts of the European Union (EU) the governments of several countries, including France and the Netherlands, have adopted action plans and targets for encouraging the conversion from conventional to organic farming. In some countries, this change has been left to market forces, which will always slow down conversion. A conventional farmer moving to organic has to endure a two-year conversion period during which time yields will drop because artificial pesticides and antibiotics are not used, yet higher prices cannot be obtained because the produce is not fully organic. Twelve of the EU member countries provide organic farmers with maintenance payments after the conversion program. Only three countries, including the UK, do not. Despite this, organic food consumption in the UK continues to grow by over 40 percent a year, an amazing statistic considering that most of this demand has to be met by importing foods.

Production of organic food is increasing rapidly in Latin America and the Pacific region, particularly in Mexico, Australia, and New Zealand. If this trend continues, and it seems certain to, we can look forward to more food being produced to organic standards.

THE RISING POPULARITY OF ORGANIC FOOD

The following statistics illustrate the explosion in popularity of organic food around Europe:

• Sales of organic fruit and vegetables are increasing by 40% a year, but in 1998, as little as just over 1% of the land farmed in the UK was farmed organically

• Organic produce accounts for around 10% of the market in Germany, Switzerland, Austria, Denmark, Finland, and Sweden; around Europe the average is about 2.5%

• Retail sales from organic food range from $18 million a year in Italy to a staggering $2.25 billion in Germany.

is well *established* in many countries

RECIPES

The pleasure of feeding your child and

being appreciated for your efforts cannot

be underestimated. These recipes have

been created to offer a variety of flavors

and textures using simple and tasty

organic ingredients.

4~7 months

MOVING ON FROM MILK

BREAST OR FORMULA MILK IS THE ONLY SUITABLE FOOD DURING THE FIRST FOUR MONTHS. AFTER THIS, YOUR BABY NEEDS SOME SOLID FOOD IN HER DIET.

At first, your baby cannot sit up or chew and cannot absorb complex foods. However, by four to seven months of age milk alone no longer meets her body's demands for nutrition and energy as she grows. This is why you need to wean your baby onto solid food. Your baby starts by consuming thicker and thicker liquids – the first solid foods are purées – and then chewing and swallowing food containing lumps. She is then ready for adapted versions of "adult" foods at the end of the weaning period.

First foods *for* your baby

FOODS TO AVOID

Exclude the following from
your baby's diet:

• Salt added to your baby's
food may strain her immature
kidneys

• Excessive sugar is associated
with tooth decay; it also passes
immediately into the
bloodstream giving quick but
unnatural energy bursts

• Wheat and rye contain gluten,
which can trigger celiac disease
in a tiny number of babies if fed
to them before 6 months of age

• Soft eggs may contain
Salmonella, a food-poisoning
bacteria

• Soft cheeses may contain
Listeria bacteria, which can
cause food poisoning

• Honey may contain botulism
spores, which can cause illness

• Nut products can, in a small
number of children, trigger a
nut allergy, which can be very
serious (see pages 136–37).

The basics of weaning

Between four and seven months of age your baby starts to show that
she is ready for solids. Many babies can sit with help, hold food in their
mouths, and mix it with saliva. They may chew anything within reach,
drool, or cry when they see food and appear hungry after milk feedings.

Once you have decided to start weaning, you can establish a regular
mealtime when you give your baby your undivided attention. Some
babies are hungriest in the morning, others in the evening.

Initially, try offering your baby small amounts of food at the end
of a spoon. Some babies eat what is offered and look around for more.
Others may protest at a spoon being placed in their mouths. The
majority swallow some food and dribble the rest down their chins.
Each day, offer your baby extra teaspoonfuls of food if she seems
hungry. About two weeks after the first meal, introduce a second.
If feeding progresses well, offer a third meal after two more weeks.

Preparing purées

For the first food, try mixing boiled rice with water, formula, or breast
milk and puréeing it to the consistency of thick soup. Alternatively, try
a pure baby rice. If this is well received, try introducing cooked, puréed
apple or pear. For a third meal, try cooked, puréed potato or carrot.

An increasing number of puréed organic fruit and vegetables are
produced commercially for babies. However, it is easy to make your own
purées. Some foods, such as banana, can be simply mashed with a fork.

**Always try to buy certified organic ingredients, particularly for
these essential first foods.**

Organic superfoods

RICE Rice is rich in protein and B vitamins and is gluten-free. Organic rice is grown without artificial pesticides.

BREAST MILK The ultimate superfood, breast milk is produced to satisfy your baby's specific needs.

Other foods can be pushed through a sieve, but a hand blender or food processor is a time saving purchase. Fibers and seeds should be removed and fruit and vegetables should be peeled before cooking and puréeing. At this age, fibrous matter is difficult for a baby to digest.

You should start to add more protein – meat, fish, cheese, yogurt, and beans – to your baby's diet. Protein should be introduced gradually, at first just once a day, to avoid straining your baby's kidneys.

Weaning around the world

In every culture, weaning aims to accustom babies to the staple diet, while relying on milk as the main source of nutrition. In countries where food is in short supply, mothers may breast feed for up to two years.

Weaning foods are universally bland and of high carbohydrate composition. In many cases, recipes for traditional weaning foods have been passed down through generations. In Asian countries, rice is the basis of kedgeree or kongi, which is fed to babies from five months of age. Initially, boiled, strained rice is added to cooked lentil juice. As babies mature, puréed lentil is added to rice; followed by peas, carrots, tomato pulp, dill, cilantro, and sometimes yogurt. Kongi, in China, is supplemented with vegetables, fish, or chicken. In the Caribbean, first foods are often steamed. For example, steamed white fish and pumpkin are puréed with cho-cho, a local vegetable. Parents also offer their babies puréed chick-----le or fish. In Africa, hot corn cereal or rice forms the first f----- -----getable and protein-rich foods are gradually added. In ----- ----- h of South America, first foods are based on potatoes, c----- ----- beans, and tortillas.

Q&A

WHY DOES MY BABY CRY AND REFUSE FOOD EVEN THOUGH I AM SURE SHE IS HUNGRY?

Your baby may not enjoy her first taste of solid food if she is very hungry. Before offering the first meal, give a short milk feeding first.

I AM RETURNING TO WORK. SHALL I SWITCH FROM BREAST TO FORMULA MILK?

This is not a good time because you are asking your baby to cope with two big changes: your absence and feeding from a bottle. It is best to make a transition from breast milk to formula milk either a couple of weeks before or after you start work.

The early weeks of weaning are a time to encourage your child to try new **TEXTURES** and **TASTES**. Here I've taken my favorite simple **VEGETABLES** and made a nutritious **BRIGHT YELLOW PURÉE**.

Baby's First Vegetables

1 tsp olive oil

1 large carrot, peeled and chopped

1 potato, peeled and chopped

1 tbsp peas, fresh or frozen

2 tbsp corn kernels, frozen or canned (unsalted)

4 tbsp water

Heat the olive oil in a small pan over medium heat. Add the carrot and fry until soft, about 5 minutes.

Add the potato, peas, corn, and water and stir to mix. Bring to a boil, then reduce the heat, cover and simmer for about 15 minutes, stirring occasionally to prevent sticking.

Purée by pushing through a sieve or by using a blender. Add a little more water if a thinner consistency is preferred.

makes	suitable for	storage	preparation	nutritional value
2–3 servings for a 4-month-old; 1 serving for a 6-month-old	vegetarians; those intolerant to gluten, milk, and lactose	24 hours in the refrigerator; 4 weeks in the freezer	15 minutes + 20 minutes cooking time	Good source of ★ complex carbohydrates ★ vitamin E

Babies need high-energy foods because they grow so rapidly. This recipe contains a tasty organic olive oil to boost its energy level.

ORGANIC APPLES are often grown from traditional varieties such as Macintoshes and Macouns. They tend to be more resistant to pests so farmers can **AVOID** the use of artificial **PESTICIDES** and fungicides.

Apple and Apricot Purée

2 small apples, peeled, cored, and finely chopped

2 peeled fresh apricots or 6 dried apricots, finely chopped

Place the apples and apricots in a pan and just cover with water.

Bring to a boil, then reduce the heat, cover and simmer for about 5 minutes. Strain the water and set aside.

Purée the fruit mixture by pushing through a sieve or by using a blender. Add a little of the reserved water if a thinner consistency is preferred.

makes	suitable for	storage	preparation	nutritional value
2–3 servings for a 4-month-old; 1 serving for a 6-month-old	vegetarians; those intolerant to gluten, milk, and lactose	24 hours in the refrigerator; 4 weeks in the freezer	10 minutes + 10 minutes cooking time	Good source of ★ vitamin A

The fresh taste of apples and apricots combined in a soft purée makes this an ideal dessert after a savory lunch.

Fruit Compote - Baby's First Christmas

⅓ cup (75ml) water

½ tbsp oats

½ small apple, peeled, cored, and finely chopped

1 peeled fresh apricot or 4 dried apricots, finely chopped

½ dried fig, chopped

pinch cinnamon

2 tsp golden raisins

Place all the ingredients in a small pan and bring to a boil over high heat. Reduce the heat, then cover and simmer for about 5 minutes, stirring occasionally to prevent sticking.

Purée the fruit mixture by pushing through a sieve or by using a blender. Add a little more water if a thinner consistency is preferred.

This is a version of **CHRISTMAS PUDDING** but without the fat and sugar of the traditional dish. Babies love it, so I also make it at other times of year – when I call it **FRUIT COMPOTE**.

makes	suitable for	storage	preparation	nutritional value
2–3 servings for a 4-month-old; 1 serving for a 6-month-old	vegetarians; those intolerant to milk and lactose	24 hours in the refrigerator; 4 weeks in the freezer	10 minutes + 5–10 minutes cooking time	Good source of ★ iron ★ vitamin C

Babies enjoy the taste and sensation of very small amounts of spices and herbs in their food – baby food should not be bland.

BERRIES add a tang to sweeter dishes and are rich in **VITAMIN C** and many **MINERALS**. This simple recipe combines the smooth texture of mashed **BANANAS** with the high **ENERGY** content of **RICE**.

Banana and Berries

4 tbsp water

½ tbsp baby rice or ground rice

1 banana, finely chopped

10 berries such as raspberries, strawberries, or blueberries, in any combination, fresh or frozen

Bring the water to a boil in a small pan. Add the remaining ingredients and simmer gently for about 5 minutes, stirring occasionally to prevent sticking.

Purée the fruit mixture by pushing through a sieve or by using a blender. Add a little more water if a thinner consistency is preferred.

makes	suitable for	storage	preparation	nutritional value
2–3 servings for a 4-month-old; 1 serving for a 6-month-old	vegetarians; those intolerant to gluten, milk, and lactose	24 hours in the refrigerator; 4 weeks in the freezer	5 minutes + 10 minutes cooking time	Good source of ★ iron ★ vitamin C

Try to use berries that have been harvested when they are in season – their nutrient levels will be much higher.

Mothers have relied on prunes over the years as a great natural aid to relieving constipation in a baby.

Fruity Hot Cereals

BANANA HOT CEREAL

½ tbsp oats

⅔ cup (150ml) water

1 small, ripe banana, mashed

2 tsp golden raisins

PRUNE AND APPLE HOT CEREAL

½ tbsp oats

⅔ cup (150ml) water

1 small apple, peeled, cored,
and chopped

4 dried prunes, finely chopped

APRICOT HOT CEREAL

½ tbsp of oats

⅔ cup (150ml) water

2 small, peeled, fresh apricots
or 5 dried apricots, finely chopped

½ tbsp golden raisins

Put all the ingredients in a small pan, cover
and bring to a boil.

Reduce the heat and simmer gently for about
5 minutes, stirring occasionally to prevent
sticking.

Purée by pushing through a sieve or by using
a blender. Add more water if a thinner
consistency is preferred.

makes 2–3 servings for a 4-month-old; 1 serving for a 7-month-old
suitable for vegetarians; those intolerant to milk and lactose
storage 24 hours in the refrigerator; 4 weeks in the freezer
preparation 10 minutes + 6 minutes cooking time
nutritional value Good source of ★ B vitamins

**Always try to buy organic bananas – there is a real difference in
the way they are grown and, I believe, in the way they taste.**

This recipe is a gentle introduction to **DAIRY** products – the cheddar cheese is just enough to give the dish a **CHEESY** flavor, without being too overpowering for your baby's palate.

Potato and Cheese Dinner

1 tsp olive oil	2 tbsp milk
½ small onion, chopped	3 tbsp water
1 potato, peeled and chopped	1 tbsp grated cheddar cheese

Heat the olive oil in a small pan over medium heat. Fry the onion until soft, about 5 minutes. Add the potato and heat gently for 1 minute.

Add the milk and water and stir to mix. Cover and simmer, stirring occasionally to prevent sticking, until the potatoes are soft, about 15 minutes. Remove from the heat and stir in the cheese until melted.

Purée by pushing through a sieve or by using a blender. Add more water if a thinner consistency is preferred.

makes	**suitable for**	**storage**	**preparation**	**nutritional value**
2–3 servings for a 4-month-old; 1 serving for a 6-month-old	vegetarians; those intolerant to gluten	24 hours in the refrigerator; 4 weeks in the freezer	15 minutes + 20 minutes cooking time	Good source of ★ calcium

Avoid adding salt to a young baby's food, and be cautious about using naturally salty foods such as cheese or smoked fish.

Tomato and Chicken Casserole

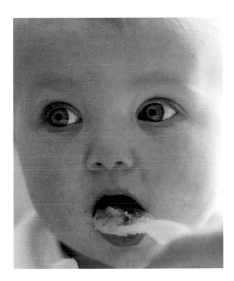

My **MOTHER**, Betty, used to make a wonderful chicken casserole for me and my sister when we were children – this is my memory of that dish, adapted for a young **BABY**.

1 tsp olive oil

1 small onion, chopped

1 carrot, peeled and chopped

pinch ground oregano

1 small potato, peeled and chopped

2 tsp peas, fresh or frozen

1 tbsp chopped chicken breast or thigh meat, raw or cooked

2 tsp tomato purée

1 tbsp Great Northern or lima beans, canned or boiled (unsalted)

5 tbsp water

Heat the olive oil in a small pan over medium heat. Fry the onion, carrot, and oregano until soft, about 5 minutes.

Add the potato, peas, chicken, tomato purée, beans, and water and stir to mix. Cover and simmer for about 20 minutes.

Purée by pushing through a sieve or by using a blender. Add more water if a thinner consistency is preferred.

makes	suitable for	storage	preparation	nutritional value
2–3 servings for a 4-month-old; 1 serving for a 6-month-old	those intolerant to gluten, milk, and lactose	24 hours in the refrigerator; 4 weeks in the freezer	15 minutes + 20 minutes cooking time	Good source of ★ iron

Nonorganic chickens are often fed with such a lot of antibiotics that they are best avoided when cooking for your baby.

RATATOUILLE,

with its soft

MEDITERRANEAN

VEGETABLES, is

a lovely meal for

a baby. This is a

version with added

chicken and root

vegetables to **BOOST**

PROTEIN and

ENERGY LEVELS.

Mediterranean Vegetables and Chicken

1 tsp olive oil

1 small onion, chopped

1 large carrot, peeled and chopped

¼ zucchini, peeled and chopped

1 mushroom, chopped

1 small strip red pepper, chopped

pinch finely chopped fresh rosemary

1 plum tomato, skinned, seeded, if desired (see below) and chopped, or 2 tsp tomato purée

1 potato, peeled and chopped

1 tbsp chopped chicken breast or thigh meat

2 tsp peas, fresh or frozen

½ cup (125ml) water

Heat the olive oil in a small pan over medium heat. Add the onion, carrot, zucchini, mushroom, red pepper, and rosemary and fry until soft, about 5 minutes.

Meanwhile, if using a plum tomato, skin and seed it: place the tomato in a heat-proof bowl, pour over boiling water to cover and let stand for 1 minute. Drain, then pour over cold water to cover. Drain again, then use a sharp knife to peel away the skin.
To seed, cut into quarters and simply scrape away the seeds.

Add the tomato or tomato purée, potato, chicken, peas, and water to the fried vegetables. Bring to a boil, then reduce the heat, cover, and simmer for about 20 minutes, stirring from time to time.

Purée by pushing through a sieve or by using a blender. For a thinner consistency, add a little more water.

makes	suitable for	storage	preparation	nutritional value
3–4 servings for a 4-month-old; 2 servings for a 6-month-old	those intolerant to gluten, milk, and lactose	24 hours in the refrigerator; 4 weeks in the freezer	15 minutes + 25 minutes cooking time	Good source of ★ iron

Vary this recipe by using fresh, seasonal vegetables. These will not have traveled so far to reach your plate.

7~10 months

NEW TEXTURES AND FLAVORS

BY SEVEN MONTHS OF AGE YOUR BABY CAN TRANSFER PIECES OF FOOD FROM HIS HAND TO HIS MOUTH, AND MAY TRY TO USE A SPOON.

Many babies now have their first teeth and can handle lumpier foods. For example, fruit and vegetables can be mashed rather than puréed, and stringier foods such as beets can be introduced. If your baby can manage these consistencies, you can try feeding him organic meat, fish, poultry, beans, and legumes. Now is also the time to introduce foods such as tiny pasta shapes, which will encourage chewing. Your baby may also begin to enjoy finger foods such as sticks of organic carrot or celery, fingers of toast, or organic baby breadsticks.

An adventure *in* eating

DIET ESSENTIALS

Babies are born with a reserve of iron, which is topped off with iron from breast or formula milk. But by the age of 6 months, these reserves start to run low, and unless babies are offered an iron-rich diet, they can become anemic, which can delay growth and development.

• Hem iron. This form of iron is most easily absorbed by your baby's digestive system and is present in red meat, poultry, liver, and oily fish.

• Nonhem iron. The vegetarian choice, nonhem iron is found in broccoli, spinach, watercress, prunes, apricots, peas, beans, and lentils. Nonhem iron is most easily absorbed when eaten with vitamin C-rich foods, such as orange juice or green vegetables.

Emerging skills and independence

At seven months of age your baby is likely to be visually alert, active, mobile, and able to transfer objects from hand to hand and from hand to mouth. He can probably roll from his back to his tummy, lift his head, sit with support, and stand while being held. He sleeps less during the day and is ready for new experiences including the taste of new textured foods and feeding himself.

By encouraging your baby to hold a spoon or a piece of food, you encourage independence and help to develop coordination. You can encourage communication skills by discussing your baby's food with him. By maintaining eye contact, smiling, saying "yum, yum" and playing games, you can establish mealtimes as happy times.

All babies are different – some eat whatever is put in front of them, others seem able to survive on next to nothing, which can make feeding time very stressful. If so, ask yourself if your baby really needs a certain type or quantity of food. After all, this new eating adventure is not only about nutrition, it is also about your baby's emerging independence and his ability to make choices about the food he likes and dislikes.

A range of new experiences

First "finger foods" could include a stick of organic carrot, a finger of toast, or a breadstick. At this stage, your baby just sucks on the food. However, as he becomes more active his appetite will increase. He watches other people eating and drinking, and wants to copy them.

By 7 months of age babies need to eat an iron-rich diet to prevent them from becoming anemic.

Many babies now have their first teeth and can handle lumpier foods. For example, apple can be grated rather than steamed and puréed. If your baby can manage these consistencies, then stringier vegetables, such as carrots, can be mashed too. This is the time to try foods such as organic fish, meat, and poultry. Make sure that you introduce meat – or legumes, such as beans and lentils – gradually.

Red meat should be offered to a nonvegetarian baby at least once a week. It is the richest and most efficiently absorbed source of iron. At first, try offering stock, for example with mashed vegetables. Once your baby is able to chew lumpier foods, you can incorporate ground meat.

Dried legumes and beans, also rich in iron, are popular with babies because of their smooth texture. Cook them thoroughly since undercooked legumes can be difficult for a baby to digest. Red and brown lentils, chickpeas, black eye beans, white, flageolet, and kidney beans are rich in carbohydrate, fiber, B vitamins, minerals, folic acid, selenium, iron, and zinc. Buy organic since residues can be present in nonorganic varieties. Cans of organic baked beans, with no added sugar or salt, are also available and make excellent pantry stand-bys.

New chewing skills mean that your baby can try cereals such as organic oatmeal accompanied by fresh puréed fruit. Or try pasta – a great food that encourages babies to chew and use their jaw muscles.

In the time that your baby continues to master eating solid food, breast or formula milk remains the most nutritionally important food. Health experts recommend that cow's milk should not yet be offered to drink. However, it is fine in cooked foods such as cauliflower and cheese or rice pudding. Organic yogurts may also be added to puréed fruit.

HOW MUCH MILK SHOULD I GIVE TO MY 7-MONTH OLD BABY?
Once your baby has established a pattern of eating, offer breast or formula milk as an after-meal drink only. This is particularly important at breakfast time. Giving food first not only encourages good eating habits, but after a night's sleep may form the largest meal. As your baby gets older he will reduce his own milk intake as his food intake increases.

WHAT TYPE OF WATER SHOULD MY BABY DRINK?
Offer either cooled, boiled tap water or sterilized, bottled water. Mineral water is not suitable for babies.

Organic superfoods

BANANAS A high-energy food that is easily digested, bananas are a rich source of vitamins B and C, potassium, magnesium, and iodine.

MEAT This provides the perfect combination of iron and zinc. Beef and lamb are richest in iron, followed by pork and chicken.

This makes a wholesome **BREAKFAST**, but it can be served at any time of day – babies love the **CREAMINESS OF OATS** and **FRUIT** mixed together.

Apple and Banana Breakfast

¾ tbsp oats
⅓ cup (75ml) water
1 small apple, peeled and finely chopped

½ small banana, mashed
½ tbsp chopped golden raisins

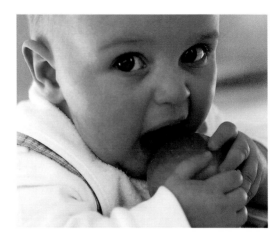

Put the oats, water, apple, and banana in a small pan and stir to mix. Bring to a boil, then reduce the heat, cover, and simmer for 5–10 minutes.

Purée by pushing through a sieve or by using a blender.

Add the raisins, then set aside until cool and the raisins are plump and soft.

makes
2 servings for a
7-month-old; 1 serving
for a 10-month-old

suitable for
vegetarians; those
intolerant to milk
and lactose

storage
24 hours in the
refrigerator; 4 weeks
in the freezer

preparation
10 minutes
+ 5–10 minutes
cooking time

nutritional value
Good source of
★ calcium

The more fruit the better – try adding berries when in season, or puréed tropical fruit for a tangy flavor.

Banana and Fig Hot Cereal

3 tbsp water

½ tbsp oats

½ dried fig, finely chopped
or puréed

1 small banana, mashed

Put the oats and the water in a small pan and bring to a boil. Cover and simmer for about 5 minutes, stirring occasionally to prevent sticking.

Remove from the heat and stir in the fig.

Put the mixture aside to cool, then add the banana and mix with a fork until well combined.

Figs add a **RICH, FRUITY TASTE** and **TEXTURE** to this recipe. Like prunes, when used carefully figs can also solve any lingering constipation as your baby adjusts from milk-only feedings.

makes
2 servings for a
7-month-old;
1 serving for a
10-month-old

suitable for
vegetarians; those
intolerant to milk
and lactose

storage
24 hours in the
refrigerator; 4 weeks
in the freezer

preparation
10 minutes
+ 5 minutes
cooking time

nutritional value
Good source of
★ magnesium
★ vitamin C

Made with tomatoes, basil, parmesan cheese, and a hint of garlic, this **TRADITIONAL PASTA SAUCE** is good served with small **PASTA SHAPES.**

Pasta with Tomato and Basil Sauce

1 tsp olive oil

½ very small onion, finely chopped

½ small celery stick, finely chopped

½ small garlic clove, chopped

¼ tsp chopped fresh basil

1 small carrot, peeled and chopped

½ small potato, peeled and chopped

2oz canned tomatoes, chopped

½ tsp cream cheese

½ tsp grated parmesan

3 tbsp water

1 tbsp pasta shapes

Heat the oil in a small pan over medium heat. Fry the onion, celery, garlic, and basil until soft, about 5 minutes. Reserve 1 tablespoon of the mixture. Add the carrot, potato, tomatoes, cream cheese, parmesan, and water to the pan. Cover and simmer for 10 minutes.

Cook the pasta according to the directions on the package and drain well. Purée or mash the sauce to a slightly lumpy texture. Stir in the reserved fried vegetables and extra water if a thinner consistency is preferred.

makes
2 servings for a
7-month-old; 1 serving
for a 10-month-old

suitable for
vegetarians; those
intolerant to gluten

storage
24 hours in the
refrigerator; 4 weeks
in the freezer

preparation
15 minutes
+ 15 minutes
cooking time

nutritional value
Good source of
★ B vitamins
★ iron

You may think that this sauce will be too strong for your child, but it is a great favorite served with the milder flavor of pasta.

Pasta with Bolognese Sauce

½ tbsp olive oil

1 small onion, finely chopped

½ celery stick, finely chopped

1 small carrot, peeled and chopped

4oz (125g) finely chopped beef

3 tomatoes, choppped, or 7oz (200g) canned chopped tomatoes

½ cup (90ml) water

1 tbsp fresh or frozen peas

pinch dried basil

1 tbsp pasta shapes

Heat the oil in a small pan over medium heat. Fry the onion, celery, and carrot for about 2 minutes, then add the chopped beef and brown for about 2 minutes.

Add the tomatoes and the water and bring to a boil. Reduce the heat, cover, and simmer for 20 minutes, stirring from time to time. Add the peas and basil and simmer for another 5 minutes.

Meanwhile, cook the pasta according to the directions on the package and drain well.

Purée or roughly mash the bolognese mixture. Add the drained pasta and mix well.

Add extra water if a thinner consistency is preferred.

This classic **PASTA SAUCE** is a wonderful way to introduce your baby to **RED MEAT,** an excellent source of dietary **IRON.**

makes	suitable for	storage	preparation	nutritional value
2 servings for a 7-month-old; 1 serving for a 10-month-old	those intolerant to gluten, milk, and lactose	24 hours in the refrigerator; 4 weeks in the freezer	15 minutes + 40 minutes cooking time	Good source of ★ iron

Don't purée these pasta sauce recipes too much – this type of meal should encourage your baby to chew.

At about 7 months babies need to start using the muscles that help them to chew and speak. Eating **TINY**, soft pieces of **PASTA** helps them to do this – making pasta an **IDEAL FOOD** for this age group.

Pasta with Tomato and Cheese Sauce

1 tsp olive oil

½ small onion, finely chopped

1 small carrot, peeled and finely chopped

very small pinch ground parsley

1 bay leaf

½ cup (125ml) strained canned tomatoes or purée

2 tbsp water

2 tsp grated cheddar cheese

1 tbsp small pasta shapes (stars, alphabets, etc.)

Heat the oil in a small pan over medium heat. Lightly fry the onion and carrot until soft, about 5 minutes. Set aside half of the mixture.

Add the parsley, bay leaf, tomatoes, or purée, and water. Cover and simmer for 10 minutes, stirring occasionally to prevent sticking. Remove from the heat, add the cheese, and stir well.

In a separate pan, cook the pasta according to the directions on the package and drain well.

Remove the bay leaf, then purée or roughly mash the tomato and cheese mixture. Add the drained pasta and reserved vegetable mixture and mix well.

Add extra water if a thinner consistency is preferred.

makes
2 servings for a 7-month-old; 1 serving for a 10-month-old

suitable for
vegetarians

storage
24 hours in the refrigerator; 4 weeks in the freezer

preparation
15 minutes + 20 minutes cooking time

nutritional value
Good source of
★ vitamin C
★ vitamin E

If the pieces of pasta are too big, you can always blend or mash them at first.

The creamy taste of **COCONUT** makes it a popular ingredient in baby food. Here, I have tried to reproduce a smooth korma by blending coconut with **MILD SPICES**, root vegetables, beans, and **TOMATO**.

Vegetable and Coconut Korma

1 tsp olive oil

½ small onion, chopped

1 small carrot, peeled and diced

pinch each of ground ginger, cumin, coriander, and turmeric

2 tsp tomato purée

1 small potato, peeled and finely diced

1 tbsp beans such as white or lima beans, canned or boiled (unsalted)

2 tsp flaked coconut

½ cup (90ml) water

Heat the oil in a small pan over medium heat. Lightly fry the onion and carrot until soft, about 5 minutes.

Add the spices and tomato purée and heat for 3 minutes, stirring continuously. Put half of the mixture in a bowl and set aside.

Add the potato, beans, coconut, and water to the pan. Bring to a boil, then reduce the heat, cover, and simmer for about 15 minutes.

Purée roughly or mash. Mix in the reserved vegetables, adding extra water if a thinner consistency is preferred.

makes	**suitable for**	**storage**	**preparation**	**nutritional value**
2 servings for a 7-month-old; 1 serving for a 10-month-old	vegetarians; those intolerant to gluten, milk, and lactose	24 hours in the refrigerator; 4 weeks in the freezer	10 minutes + 25 minutes cooking time	Good source of ★ iron ★ magnesium

Use any combination of green beans and root vegetables in this dish. All these new flavors are a great adventure for your baby.

Corn and Potato

1 tsp olive oil

½ very small onion, finely chopped

1 small carrot, peeled and finely chopped

½ cup (90ml) water

1 small potato, peeled and chopped

3 tbsp corn kernels from fresh or frozen cobs

 tsp chopped fresh herbs such as basil, oregano, or thyme

Heat the oil in a small pan over medium heat. Lightly fry the onion and carrot until soft, about 5 minutes. Put half of this mixture in a bowl and set aside.

Add the water, potato, and corn to the pan and stir to mix. Cover and simmer for about 15 minutes.

Add the herbs, then purée or roughly mash the mixture before adding the reserved vegetables. Add extra water if a thinner consistency is preferred.

Introduce your baby's eager taste buds to the new and **EXCITING FLAVORS** of **CORN** and fresh **HERBS** with this simple, delicious **PURÉE**.

makes	suitable for	storage	preparation	nutritional value
2 servings for a 7-month-old; 1 serving for a 10-month-old	vegetarians; those intolerant to gluten, milk, and lactose	24 hours in the refrigerator; 4 weeks in the freezer	10 minutes + 20 minutes cooking time	Good source of ★ complex carbohydrates

This is a **DELICIOUS**

COMBINATION of

fruit with chicken

and rice – a

NUTRITIOUS BLEND

that I first saw fed

to babies in **NORTH**

AFRICA. This

version has fewer

SPICES and less

DRIED FRUIT.

Fruity Rice with Chicken and Apricot

1 tsp olive oil

½ small onion, chopped

1 small peeled fresh apricot, or 2 dried apricots, chopped

1 tbsp chicken breast or thigh meat, raw or cooked

1 plum tomato, skinned, seeded, if desired (see page 42), and chopped, or 2 tsp tomato purée

2 tsp golden raisins

¼ tsp finely chopped fresh rosemary

pinch each ground coriander and cinnamon

¼ tsp finely chopped garlic

½ cup (90ml) water

1 tbsp basmati rice

Heat the oil in a small pan over medium heat. Add the onion and fry until soft, about 2 minutes.

Mix in the apricot, chicken, tomato or tomato purée, and raisins.

Add the herbs, spices, garlic, and water. Bring to a boil, then reduce the heat, cover, and simmer for about 20 minutes, stirring occasionally to prevent sticking.

In a separate pan, boil the rice according to the package instructions.

Add half of the cooked rice to the pan and reserve the rest.

Roughly purée or mash the fruity mixture, then add the reserved rice and mix well. If your child is not used to lumpy food, you may want to purée the whole meal in a blender. Add extra water if a thinner consistency is preferred.

makes
2 servings for a 7-month-old; 1 serving for a 10-month-old

suitable for
those intolerant to gluten, milk, and lactose

storage
24 hours in the refrigerator; 4 weeks in the freezer

preparation
15 minutes + 20 minutes cooking time

nutritional value
Good source of ★ calcium

Try serving this dish with couscous instead of rice – your baby may prefer the smaller grains.

Made with apple, **JUICY CHERRIES,** and the sweetest **SEASONAL BERRIES,** this is a **DELICIOUS** vitamin-rich dessert.

Berries and Cherries

⅓ cup oz (75ml) water

1 tsp ground rice

1 tsp basmati rice

1 large apple, peeled, cored, and finely chopped

4 raspberries

1–2 strawberries

2 cherries, pitted and chopped

Bring the water to a boil in a small pan. Add the ground and basmati rice, cover, and simmer for about 10 minutes, stirring occasionally to prevent sticking.

Add the fruit and simmer until the apple is soft, about 10 minutes.

Purée by pushing through a sieve or by mashing the fruit with a fork. Add extra water if a thinner consistency is preferred.

makes	suitable for	storage	preparation	nutritional value
2 servings for a 7-month-old; 1 serving for a 10-month-old	vegetarians; those intolerant to gluten, milk, and lactose	24 hours in the refrigerator; 4 weeks in the freezer	5 minutes + 20 minutes cooking time	Good source of ★ iron ★ vitamin C

Use any soft berries in this purée – seasonal ones will taste the best. Lightly cook the fruit to preserve its vitamin content.

In this **DELECTABLE** rice pudding, the fresh, tangy taste of **APRICOTS** is offset by the **SWEETER** flavor of **RAISINS**.

Rice Pudding with Apricots

⅓ cup (75ml) water

1 tbsp ground rice

1 tsp basmati or white short-grain rice

1–2 fresh apricots, peeled, or 6 dried apricots, finely chopped

1 tsp golden raisins

2 tsp plain yogurt

Bring the water to a boil in a small pan. Add the ground and basmati or short-grain rice and simmer gently for 5 minutes, stirring occasionally to prevent sticking.

Add the apricots and raisins and simmer for about 5 minutes. Use a slotted spoon to set aside about a tablespoon of this mixture.

Purée the rest of the mixture by pushing through a sieve or by using a blender. Stir in the reserved mixture, the yogurt, and water if a thinner consistency is preferred.

makes
2 servings for a 7-month-old; 1 serving for a 10-month-old

suitable for
vegetarians; those intolerant to gluten

storage
24 hours in the refrigerator; 4 weeks in the freezer

preparation
5 minutes + 10 minutes cooking time

nutritional value
Good source of ★ vitamin A

You can use any type of natural yogurt, but whole milk yogurt is best for your child since it is the most energy-dense.

Banana and Mango Coulis

⅓ cup (75ml) water
1 tbsp ground rice
½ juicy ripe mango
1 small banana

Bring the water to a boil in a small pan. Add the rice, cover, and simmer very gently for about 5 minutes, stirring occasionally to prevent sticking. Remove from the heat and set aside to cool to just above room temperature.

Purée the mango and half of the banana in a blender, or by pushing it through a sieve.

Combine the purée with the rice and serve with the remaining banana pieces.

Mangoes with their **VELVETY** flesh, rich yellow color and distinctive **AROMATIC** smell are a **DELIGHT** for a baby. Organic mangoes will have been grown without artificial pesticides.

makes
2 servings for a 7-month-old; 1 serving for a 10-month-old

suitable for
vegetarians; those intolerant to gluten, milk, and lactose

storage
24 hours in the refrigerator; 4 weeks In the freezer

preparation
5 minutes + 20 minutes cooking time

nutritional value
Good source of
★ vitamin C

10~15 months

HEALTHY MEALS AND SNACKS

THIS IS A TIME OF DISCOVERY, NEW SKILLS, AND BEING ENCOURAGED BY YOU. THE KEY TO ALL THIS LEARNING IS PLAY – MUCH OF WHICH CAN HAPPEN AT MEALTIMES.

At around ten months your baby will be beginning to stand, holding on to the furniture or to you. He will soon stand alone and will take his first steps by about 15 months. He can now fit cubes into boxes, place rings on a stick, throw a ball, and build a small tower. By 15 months many babies can say single words, and some may produce two-word sentences. Some babies will still be breast-fed and some may be taking milk from a bottle. If you have not already done so, try introducing a cup.

Feeding *your* older baby

NEW FLAVORS

Herbs have nutritional and therapeutic properties as well as enhancing the taste of food. Introducing them into your child's diet now encourages a love of variety and emphasizes that "flavoring" should come from natural rather than heavily processed ingredients. Nonorganic herbs are sometimes grown hydroponically (in a chemical solution with no soil), which means that they can have poor nutrient and essential oil levels. Buy organic herbs (see pages 140–41), and try growing some of the following at home, in the garden or in a window box:

• Parsley is very rich in vitamins A and C as well as iron, calcium, and potassium

• Cilantro is widely used in Asian weaning cuisine since it supplies essential oils beneficial to the digestive system

• Basil and oregano are rich in essential oils; basil is soothing and oregano can be invigorating.

Encouraging healthy snacking habits

Babies now have several teeth, which means that they can chew. Teeth brushing can be introduced as a game to be played each morning and evening, but it has a serious purpose – to establish the routine. You might want to find out about the fluoride status of the water in your area. Since fluoride supplementation can be controversial, ask your doctor or dentist if you should choose a baby toothpaste with fluoride.

You will be bombarded with snack foods for children, from cookies and potato chips to candies and yogurts, but while your baby is still too young to be influenced by peer pressure, you can encourage him to snack on fruit or simple savories rather than sweets or heavily processed snacks. This helps to protect those precious first teeth and ensures that your baby gets the nutrition he needs. It also helps to develop a taste for healthier, less processed foods, which can become a lifetime habit.

Fruit and vegetables, rich in beta carotene, flavenoids, vitamin C, and potassium, make healthy snacks. However, nonorganic produce may be treated with synthetic insecticides, herbicides, and fungicides, or waxed to increase its shelf life. Tests by government agencies have found pesticide residues in a good share of nonorganic fruits. Although organic fruits may not always look as good as the seemingly perfect nonorganic fruits with shiny surfaces and blemish-free skin, they often taste so much better. You may have to pay a little extra, but seeking out the organic option is one way to be sure that you are giving the best to your baby.

Dried fruits or simple savory crackers are a good alternative to sweets and make a nutritious snack for your baby.

Organic superfoods

FISH Two portions of organic fish a week give your baby all the Omega 3 oil he needs.

DRIED FRUITS Dried apricots are a good source of carotene, potassium, iron, and fiber. Prunes contain vitamin B6.

New foods to introduce

Fish is rich in Omega 3 oil, vital to brain and nervous tissue development. Indeed, Australian research has revealed that those in lower IQ brackets eat less oily fish than those in higher brackets. Fish such as sardines, mackerel, and tuna contain other essential nutrients such as vitamins B and D, iron, zinc, and iodine. Nonorganic farmed fish has been found to contain traces of antibiotics and other residues.

Introduce some of the wide range of dried fruits available, including dates, figs, mango, pineapple, papaya, and banana. However, unless they are organic they will have been treated with oils and preservatives and may also have been dipped in sugar and fried. One of the common treatments is to expose dried fruits to sulphur dioxide to preserve their color. This can have detrimental effects on children, especially those prone to suffering from asthma. Organic alternatives are darker in color than nonorganic fruits, but this is a sign of their superiority.

Onions, garlic, and leeks add lots of flavor to your baby's food. Onions are a rich source of vitamin C and scallions are also a good source of iron. Garlic has been traditionally associated with developing resistance to infection. Leeks are full of vitamins A, C, folic acid, and potassium. However, the onion family may be heavily sprayed: an average onion may receive one burst of insecticide, five of herbicides, and two of fungicides. Onions may also be treated with a growth regulator and, when harvested, with a sprout suppressant, so choose organic every time.

Unprocessed oats can lower cholesterol, stabilize blood sugar, and are rich in vitamins B and E, calcium, magnesium, and silicon. Organic oats are grown without synthetic herbicides, insecticides, and fungicides.

MY BABY DOES NOT WEIGH AS MUCH AS SOME OF MY FRIENDS' CHILDREN. HOW DO I KNOW IF HE IS GROWING NORMALLY?

It is not a good idea to compare your child with others. Take more notice of the growth chart your pediatrician can plot for you which will show your baby's real progress.

MY BABY IS EASILY DISTRACTED WHEN I'M TRYING TO FEED HIM OR TEACH HIM SOMETHING. IS SOMETHING WRONG?

Only a tiny minority of children suffer from conditions such as hyperactivity and attention deficit disorder, and these symptoms can sometimes be alleviated by changes to the diet. Your pediatrician will be able to advise you.

Breakfast Surprise

2 tbsp oats

3 tbsp each of milk and water

1 tbsp plain yogurt

⅓ cup (75g) raisins or other dried fruit, finely chopped

1 small apple

This is a version of the original Bircher Benner Swiss Muesli omitting the nuts and using **OATS** instead of wheat flakes. The use of natural **YOGURT** adds to its nutrient value and aids the digestive process.

Combine all of the ingredients, except the apple, in a bowl, cover and store in the refrigerator overnight.

Before serving, grate the apple and stir into the oat mixture.

Serve cold in the summer, or heat gently for a warming winter breakfast.

makes
2 large servings for
a 15-month-old or
1 adult serving

suitable for
vegetarians

storage
24 hours in
the refrigerator

preparation
5 minutes + overnight
refrigeration

nutritional value
Good source of
★ calcium
★ vitamin D

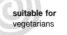

Add mashed, fresh berries or diced, fresh peaches to make this a sunny, summer breakfast.

Mixed Fruit Compote

½ cup (60g) strawberries, chopped

⅓ cup (60g) raspberries

2 dried apricots, finely chopped

1 dried prune or fig, finely chopped

1 peach or nectarine, pitted and chopped

1 kiwi fruit, chopped

1 small apple or pear, cored and chopped

¼ cup (125ml) orange or grapefruit juice (unsweetened)

pinch ground ginger

Place the prepared fruit in a large bowl, and stir to mix. In a separate bowl, mix together the fruit juice and ginger. Pour the mixture over the fruit, stir, and let stand for a few minutes to help the flavors blend.

Warm gently before serving or pour the compote into warm bowls.

A delicious way of eating **FRESH FRUIT**, this compote makes enough for all the family. The **SECRET** is in combining both soft and hard fruits in a citrus juice that is lifted lightly with a pinch of **GINGER**.

makes
8 servings for a 15-month-old or 2 child and 2 adult servings

suitable for
vegetarians; those intolerant to gluten, milk, and lactose

storage
eat immediately

preparation
10 minutes

nutritional value
Good source of
★ Iron
★ vitamin C

If you cannot find **ORGANIC FISH**, try to buy **WILD** rather than farmed fish. Serve these fish cakes with green beans, halved tomatoes, and a puréed root vegetable such as turnip.

Fish Cakes

2 large potatoes, cut into chunks

1 tbsp fresh lemon juice

2 tbs (30g) butter

7oz (200g) fresh white or pink fish such as cod or salmon, bones and skin removed, or 1 x 7oz (200g) can salmon or tuna in oil or spring water, drained

milk for poaching

6 scallions, trimmed and chopped

freshly ground black pepper

a little flour to prevent sticking

1 egg

2 tbsp milk

1 heaping cup (90g) fresh breadcrumbs

3 tbsp good quality vegetable oil

Cook the potatoes in a pan of boiling water until soft, about 12–15 minutes. Drain, and mash with the lemon juice and half of the butter.

If using fresh fish, poach it in a pan of milk: add enough milk to cover the fish, bring to a boil, then reduce the heat and simmer until the fish is no longer translucent, about 5–10 minutes. Drain the fish and chop into small pieces.

In a separate pan, fry the scallions in the remaining butter until soft. Add the scallions, fish, and pepper to the potato mixture and combine. Divide the mixture into 8, and pat into burger shapes with floured hands.

Beat the egg and milk together in a bowl. Coat each burger first in the egg mixture, then in the breadcrumbs.

Heat half of the oil in a frying pan over medium heat, then turn the heat down to low and add 4 burgers. Fry, turning once, until golden brown, about 5 minutes on each side. Drain on paper towel and keep warm. Add the rest of the oil and repeat the process with the remaining burgers.

makes
8 rissoles

suitable for
fish-eating vegetarians

storage
freeze when cool and use within 1 week

preparation
25 minutes
+ 35 minutes
cooking time

nutritional value
Good source of
★ B vitamins
★ vitamin D

You could ask your fish seller to remove the fish bones and skin for you, and cut the fish into chunks.

Most young children like **PASTA** and **SAUCE**. With so many shapes available, from **MINI-ALPHABETS** to **ANIMALS**, it should be easy to find one that your child enjoys eating.

Pasta with Creamy Mushroom Sauce

1 tsp olive oil

½ small onion, finely chopped

6 small button mushrooms, finely chopped

½ small garlic clove, crushed

1 small potato, chopped

2 tbsp milk

3 tbsp water

1 tbsp small pasta shapes

1 tsp chopped fresh parsley

Heat the oil in a pan over medium heat. Fry the onion, mushrooms, and garlic until soft, about 5 minutes. Reserve one-third of this mixture. Add the potato, milk, and water to the pan and bring to a boil. Reduce the heat, cover, and simmer for 10 minutes, stirring occasionally.

Cook the pasta according to the directions on the package and drain well. Roughly purée the sauce in a blender, or mash to a slightly lumpy texture with a fork. Add the reserved fried vegetables, parsley, and more water if a thinner consistency is preferred.

makes
1 serving for a
15-month-old

suitable for
vegetarians

storage
24 hours in
the refrigerator

preparation
15 minutes

nutritional value
Good source of
★ vitamin C
★ vitamin E

Beef Casserole

2 tbsp good-quality vegetable oil

2 onions, sliced

1 tsp paprika

1½ lb (750g) stewing beef, cut into bite-sized pieces

¼ cup (30g) plain flour seasoned with salt and pepper

1 x 13oz (400g) can chopped tomatoes

1 large potatoe, cut into chunks

4 carrots, cut into chunks

⅔ cup (150ml) water

¼ pound (125g) squash, pumpkin, eggplant, or peas, optional

This is a traditional casserole made with **BEEF, ROOT VEGETABLES,** and **SPICES.** Serve with rice or noodles, or with baked potatoes and stir-fried shredded cabbage or sliced peppers.

This can be cooked on the stove top or in the oven. If using the oven, preheat to 325°F (160°C).

Heat the oil in a large pan over medium heat. Add the onions and fry until soft, about 5 minutes.

Add the paprika and stir fry for 30 seconds. Toss the meat in the seasoned flour and add to the pan; stir for a few minutes while the meat browns.

Add the tomatoes, potatoes, carrots, and water and bring to a boil. Reduce the heat, cover, and simmer for 1½–2 hours either on the stove top or in a preheated oven.

Add the squash, pumpkin, eggplant, or peas, if using, for the last 10–15 minutes of cooking.

makes
2 servings for a
15-month-old and
2 adult servings

suitable for
those intolerant
to milk and lactose

storage
freeze when cool and
use within 4 weeks

preparation
20 minutes
+ 1½–2 hours
cooking time

nutritional value
Good source of
★ B vitamins
★ iron
★ vitamin A

Organic beef has a great flavor and will not have been treated with the growth stimulants used on conventionally reared animals.

Meatballs are popular with most children. They can be mixed with **CREAMY CHEESE,** **VEGETABLE,** or **TOMATO SAUCES.** Here I keep it **SIMPLE** and serve them with a classic fresh tomato sauce.

Mini Meatballs in Herby Tomato Sauce

FOR MEATBALLS:

½ lb (250g) lean minced pork, lamb, or beef

½ small onion, finely chopped

1 cup (60g) mushrooms, finely chopped

2 tsp finely chopped fresh herbs such as parsley or thyme

½ cup (30g) fresh whole wheat breadcrumbs

1 egg yolk

1 tbsp good-quality vegetable oil

FOR TOMATO SAUCE:

1 large (250g) fresh tomato, skinned, seeded (see page 42), and chopped

⅔ cup (150ml) water or vegetable stock

½ small onion, finely chopped

1 tbsp tomato purée

1 tbsp finely chopped fresh herbs such as basil, parsley, or thyme

Preheat the oven to 350°F (180°C).

For the meatballs, place all the ingredients, except the oil, in a bowl and mix thoroughly. Use your hands to divide and shape the mixture into 25 balls. Chill in the refrigerator while you make the sauce.

For the sauce, put all the ingredients in a pan and bring to a boil over medium heat. Reduce the heat, cover, and simmer for about 15 minutes, stirring occasionally. Remove from the heat and let cool slightly, then blend.

Heat the oil in a frying pan over medium heat. Fry the meatballs, turning them frequently, until they are lightly browned all over, about 5–10 minutes. Put the meatballs in an ovenproof dish.

Pour the sauce over the meatballs, cover with a lid or foil and bake in the oven for about 45 minutes.

makes
25 small meatballs

suitable for
those intolerant
to milk and lactose

storage
freeze when cool and
use within 1 week

preparation
30 minutes
+ 45 minutes
cooking time

nutritional value
Good source of
★ B vitamins
★ iron

You can introduce more texture by serving the meatballs with steamed or stir-fried crunchy vegetables.

PUMPKINS seem to be grown especially for children. They have such **FUNNY SHAPES** and **BRIGHT COLORS** and look like abandoned **TOYS** in the fields at **HARVEST TIME**.

Pumpkin Stew-in-a-Pot

1 pumpkin or squash, about 6 lb (3kg)

3 tbsp good-quality vegetable oil

1lb (500g) ground pork or beef, or cooked unsalted beans such as Great Northern or lima beans

1 large (250g) onion, chopped

3 cooking apples, cored and cut into large chunks

½ cup (125ml) water or stock

⅓ cup (60g) raisins

1 tsp chopped fresh or ½ tsp dried basil or thyme

Preheat the oven to 350°F (180°C).

Cut the top off the pumpkin or squash and discard. Cut the pumpkin or squash into quarters and scoop out and discard the seeds and stringy pulp. Place the pumpkin or squash pieces cut-side down in a large, deep baking dish with ½ in (1cm) of water in the bottom. Cover with foil and bake in the oven until tender, about 2 hours.

Heat the oil in a pan and fry the meat or beans, onion, and apple until tender, about 15 minutes. Add the remaining ingredients, cover, and bring to a boil. Reduce the heat, then simmer for about 30 minutes, stirring occasionally to prevent sticking.

Drain the water from the pumpkin or squash. Use a spoon to scoop out the soft flesh, then discard the skin. Mix the flesh with the meat or bean mixture and return it to the baking dish. Cover with foil and return it to the oven until hot, about 20 minutes.

makes
4 servings for a 15-month-old

suitable for
those intolerant to gluten, milk, and lactose

storage
best eaten on day of cooking

preparation
10 minutes
+ 2 hours 20 minutes cooking time

nutritional value
Good source of
★ B vitamins
★ iron
★ vitamin A

Substitute winter squash for a sweeter flavored squash such as dumpling or acorn.

Try baking sweet potatoes for a really delicious meal that will also be rich in beta carotene.

Baked Potato Fillings

1 potato or sweet potato

FILLINGS

Hummus (see page 97)
and chopped apple

Avocado Dip (see page 78)

Vegetable and Coconut Korma (see page 54)

Dahl (see page 110)
with chopped tomato

Brussels sprouts,
tuna fish, and
a little olive oil

Mashed boiled egg

Baked beans
and cream cheese

Diced or shredded chicken with sliced red
and green peppers and a little butter

Onion,
mushroom,
and zucchini fried in a little oil
with goat's cheese

Preheat the oven to 350°F (180°C).

Prick the potato all over and bake in the oven
for 30–60 minutes, depending on the size of
the potato.

Serve with any filling – each one makes a
complete nutritionally balanced meal.

makes 1 serving per potato
suitable for check individual recipes; those intolerant to milk
and lactose should avoid cheese fillings
storage 24 hours in the refrigerator
preparation approximately 10–15 minutes, but check individual
recipes, + 30–60 minutes cooking time
nutritional value Potatoes are a good source of ★ vitamin B
★ vitamin C ★ potassium. Sweet potatoes are a good source of
★ vitamin C ★ vitamin E ★ magnesium.

*Cooking potatoes in their skins retains their high levels of
potassium and vitamins B and C.*

Avocado's **RICH, CREAMY** texture makes it a great food for babies. Be sure to choose a soft, **RIPE** avocado for this recipe. Serve with lightly steamed sticks of carrot or zucchini, or with strips of pita bread.

Avocado Dip

½ ripe avocado

2 tbs (30g) cream cheese

1 tbsp finely chopped fresh plum tomato

2 tsp plain yogurt

½ tsp finely chopped fresh mint or thyme

Blend all the ingredients in a blender or mash together with a fork.

| **makes** 1 serving for a 15-month-old | **suitable for** vegetarians | **storage** 4 hours in the refrigerator, but best eaten immediately | **preparation** 5–10 minutes | **nutritional value** Good source of ★ B vitamins ★ vitamin E |

Blending avocado with cheese, yogurt, and tomato boosts the calcium and vitamin content of this dip.

Days Out Cakes

½ pint (300ml) plain yogurt

¼ cup (30g) whole wheat flour

1 egg, beaten

½ tsp baking soda

½ cup (45g) polenta (cornmeal)

a little butter or olive oil for frying

Mix together all the ingredients except the butter or olive oil in the order listed until the batter is smooth.

Lightly coat a frying pan with the butter or olive oil, and warm over medium heat. Drop a tablespoon of the batter into the pan and fry as though making pancakes. Fry until golden, about 2 minutes on the first side and another minute on the second.

Transfer to a plate to cool, and repeat the process with the remaining batter.

These **NUTRITIOUS** cakes are based on a pancake recipe. I particularly like the use of **POLENTA,** which gives the cakes their **SPECIAL TEXTURE**. Spread them with cream cheese or fruit, and roll into wraps.

makes	suitable for	storage	preparation	nutritional value
10 cakes	vegetarians	2 days in the refrigerator; 4 weeks in the freezer	10 minutes + 20 minutes cooking time	Good source of ★ calcium ★ iron

These cakes make a good alternative to sandwiches and are much less messy to eat. Try them as a snack on car trips.

WHOLESOME breadsticks are a **NATURAL** way to introduce your child to **FINGER FOODS** without the added sugar and flavorings of commercial rusks.

Breadsticks

2 cups (50g) strong bread flour (brown or white)
1 tsp active dry yeast
1 tsp sugar
⅔ cup (150ml) warm water
2½ tsp salt

Measure the flour into a mixing bowl, add the remaining ingredients and mix until the dough is soft, smooth, and comes away from the sides of the bowl.

Turn the dough onto a lightly floured work surface and knead for about 2 minutes, adding more flour, if necessary, to prevent sticking. Return it to the bowl, cover with a damp kitchen towel, plate or plastic wrap, and let rise at room temperature until doubled in size, about 1 hour.

Preheat the oven to 375°F (190°C).

Turn the dough onto the floured surface and knead for a few minutes, adding more flour, if necessary. Divide into 30 small plum-sized pieces. Roll each piece into a long, thin stick using your palms. Cut into smaller sticks, if desired. Place the sticks on a greased baking sheet and leave in a warm place for another 20 minutes.

Bake in the oven for about 15–20 minutes. Cool on a baking rack.

makes
30 x 18cm (7in)
breadsticks

suitable for
vegetarians; those
intolerant to milk
and lactose

storage
1 week in an
airtight container

preparation
10 minutes
excluding waiting
time + 20 minutes
cooking time

nutritional value
Good source of
★ calcium
★ iron

For fruity breadsticks, add a handful of dried fruit such as currants, chopped apricots, or figs to the dough at the first kneading.

BAKING BANANAS releases their full flavor and changes their texture to an **IRRESISTIBLE GOOEY PURÉE.** Serve with yogurt, a drizzle of honey, and flaked almonds if there is no history of nut allergy.

Baked Bananas

Whole, unpeeled bananas
(not green, but not too ripe) –
1 per person

Preheat the oven to 350°F (180°C).

Place the bananas on a baking tray and bake for 25 minutes.

Remove from the oven. Allow to cool a little, then peel.

makes
1 serving per banana

suitable for
vegetarians; those
intolerant to gluten

storage
eat immediately

preparation
5 minutes
+ 25 minutes
cooking time

nutritional value
Good source of
★ vitamin C

Nuts are a nutritious addition to this recipe but must be used with care given the increasing incidence of nut allergies.

Toddler

INDEPENDENT FOOD CHOICES

BETWEEN 15 MONTHS AND TWO YEARS, YOUR BABY'S PHYSICAL, INTELLECTUAL, EMOTIONAL, AND SOCIAL DEVELOPMENT BRING WELCOME INDEPENDENCE.

The average two-year-old can walk confidently, ride a tricycle, put on socks, and complete jigsaws. By the age of two years, many children can articulate their needs and protests and can engage in dialogue. Remember that your toddler will copy what you do, not what you say.

Between one and two years, she will interpret being offered family food as a sign that she is one of the family. The emotional and nutritional needs of toddlers cannot be separated.

Changing tastes *and* eating skills

CONVENIENCE FOODS

Convenience meals usually contain preservatives, additives, fillers, and poor-quality fat or sugar which replace more nutritious ingredients. There are plenty of organic convenience foods:

• Pasta and sauce: children like the taste and texture of pasta, especially combined with their favorite sauce

• Milk: 2 cups of milk a day provide essential protein, fat, vitamins, and minerals; supermarkets sell organic milk; give toddlers the whole milk variety to fuel their rapid growth; children who are lactose-intolerant can drink fortified soy milk

• Yogurt: add chopped cucumber and mint, and serve with pita bread for a delicious lunch; serve it with chopped fruit as an evening dessert

• Cheese: this is a popular finger food for toddlers; serve it on toast or baked potatoes.

A time of burgeoning independence

Your toddler experiences tumultuous emotional changes throughout her second year. There is good reason for this being known as The Terrible Two's. While on one hand your child has acquired new skills and independence, on the other hand she is still emotionally dependent on you. She is sometimes clingy and anxious if separated from you for any length of time.

This period of change is a challenge to parents. As your child becomes more independent you have to learn to release control and allow your developing toddler to make choices, learn from mistakes and understand that her actions have consequences. This is the well-recognized process of separation.

Nowhere is this more amply illustrated than in your toddler's changing food habits and eating skills. In many ways life was easy when your baby was in her highchair and you fed her with her food. An independent-minded toddler is free to leave the table and has clear opinions about likes and dislikes – which may seem to you to be completely without logic.

A strategic approach is needed to cope with this stage of your toddler's development. Decide what you will and will not encourage or tolerate, and set your own boundaries. This will help your child to develop greater confidence, and turn what could be a time of anxiety into a time of adventure and learning. A positive, encouraging environment produces a happy and confident toddler.

Why not let your toddler help you to bake delicious homemade bread.

Bread and potatoes

Rich in fiber, bread is a good source of iron, vitamins B and E, and protein. In conventional bread the grains have been subjected to a range of artificial pesticides both during and after harvesting. During baking, flour improvers and a range of other preservatives may be added.

When choosing organic bread, look for a label that confirms that it has been certified organic. If you have difficulty finding a good loaf, you could try baking your own. Although time consuming, it can be fun if you get your child involved. Alternatively, invest in an inexpensive bread machine – they make delicious loaves, particularly if you add dried fruits, herbs, nuts, seeds, or grated citrus zest. One final point – toddlers sometimes prefer simple white bread. Do not get into a battle if that is your child's choice; respect your child's wishes and try something new a month or two later.

Potatoes, a staple of the diet in many cultures, are highly nutritious. However, the nonorganic varieties are repeatedly treated with artificial insecticides, herbicides, and fungicides, as well as growth regulators, while they are in storage. They retain pesticide residues in their skins because they are in contact with them for longer while in the earth. For this reason, governments advise parents to peel nonorganic root vegetables before serving them to children.

Q&A

WHAT SHOULD I DO WHEN MY TODDLER HAS A TANTRUM IN THE STORE OVER A CHOCOLATE BAR?

Learn to negotiate. Don't say "no," and walk away, but don't give in to make life easy. Distract your child by involving her in something else. Remind her that she can have a treat after lunch. Stay calm, despite feeling stressed.

SHOULD I INSIST THAT MY CHILD CLEANS HER PLATE?

It is more important to respect your toddler's appetite. This allows her to eat to satisfy her hunger and gives her a sense of autonomy. Praise her for the quantity eaten, and do not scold when food is unfinished.

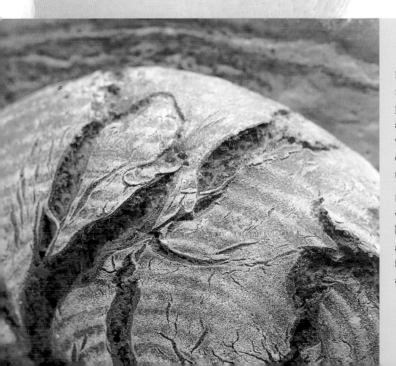

Organic superfoods

POTATOES High in fiber and rich in vitamins B and C and potassium, as long as potatoes are organic, and therefore grown without pesticides, they are best cooked in their skins for maximum nourishment.

BREAD A good source of iron, vitamins B and E, and protein, bread is also rich in fiber. It is available in so many shapes and forms that you could introduce a new variety every day.

This recipe combines **ORANGES** with **APPLES**, creamy oats, yogurt, and **PLUMP GOLDEN RAISINS** in my own version of a **HEALTHY** Swiss-style breakfast.

Apple and Orange Breakfast

freshly squeezed juice of 1½ oranges, or 4 tbsp unsweetened orange juice

½ tbsp oats

1 apple, cored and chopped

1 tsp plain yogurt

small handful golden raisins

Heat the orange juice and oats in a small pan and simmer for 5 minutes. Add the apple and simmer until soft, about 5 minutes.

Remove from the heat and stir in the yogurt.

Add the raisins and leave for a few minutes to plump up.

makes
1 child-sized
serving

suitable for
vegetarians

storage
best eaten
immediately

preparation
5 minutes
+ 10 minutes
cooking time

nutritional value
Good source of
★ vitamin C

For a stronger orange flavor, add a tablespoon of grated orange zest to the oats while they are cooking.

Fruit Bread Fingers

¼ cup (60g) good-quality vegetable oil, butter, or margarine

½ cup (125g) honey

1 egg, beaten

¾ cup (125g) carrots or apples, grated

2 small bananas, mashed

⅔ cup (90g) self-rising flour

½ cup (60g) raisins, dried cherries, or cranberries

1 tsp lemon or orange zest, finely grated and chopped

Preheat the oven to 350°F (180°C).

Cream the oil, butter or margarine with the honey in a mixing bowl. Gradually beat in the egg. Mix in the carrots or apples, bananas, and flour; add the raisins, cherries, or cranberries and zest. Add a little extra flour, if necessary, until a spoon stands upright in the mixture.

Turn the mixture into a greased 7in (18cm) shallow, square cake pan and level the surface. Bake until golden brown, about 45 minutes.

Cool slightly, then lightly score into finger-shaped slices using a sharp knife. Cool completely in the pan, then cut into fingers to serve.

A tasty **FRUIT BREAD** makes an ideal quick **BREAKFAST** or a **SNACK** to beat hunger pangs. This one combines grated **APPLES** or **CARROTS** with **DRIED FRUIT** and **CITRUS ZEST.**

	suitable for	storage	preparation	nutritional value
makes 10 fingers	vegetarians; those intolerant to milk and lactose	4 days in an airtight container, 1 week in the freezer	10 minutes + 45 minutes cooking time	Good source of ★ iron

These moist fruitcake fingers are tasty and nutritious and are sweetened naturally with honey, not sugar.

Lima beans make a **CREAMY, WHITE PURÉE** to which I add red vegetables for **TASTE** and **TEXTURE**. This is a warming dish for cold winter evenings and is delicious served with crusty bread and a salad.

Roasted Lima Bean Gratin

1 tsp good-quality vegetable oil

1 small leek, well washed and finely chopped

½ small carrot, grated

½ tsp crushed garlic

2 tbsp canned or cooked lima beans, rinsed and drained

⅔ cup (150ml) water or stock

1 tsp finely chopped fresh parsley, thyme, or basil

¼ red pepper, finely chopped

1 tomato, cut into thin rings

½ cup (60g) cheddar cheese, grated

½ cup (30g) breadcrumbs

Preheat the oven to 350°F (180°C).

Heat the oil in a pan over medium heat. Add the leek and carrot and fry gently for about 5 minutes. Add the garlic and lima beans and cook, stirring occasionally, for another 5 minutes. Add the water or stock and herbs.

Purée the mixture in a blender, then pour into an ovenproof dish and mix in the red pepper. Arrange the tomato rings on top. Mix the cheese with the breadcrumbs, and sprinkle over the top. Bake in the oven until golden brown and bubbling hot, about 20 minutes.

makes
2 child-sized servings;
1 adult serving

suitable for
vegetarians; those
intolerant to gluten

storage
24 hours in the
refrigerator; 1 week
in the freezer

preparation
15 minutes
+ 20 minutes
cooking time

nutritional value
Good source of
★ iron

Try adding diced parsnip or turnip instead of carrot. Ground ginger works well either with, or instead of, the garlic.

Lean **LAMB** is a **NUTRITIOUS** meat for young children and works very well with **ROOT VEGETABLES** and **SQUASH**. Serve this with steamed green vegetables such as **GREEN BEANS**, **BROCCOLI**, or **SNOW PEAS** and rice, couscous, or mashed potatoes.

Mediterranean Lamb

6oz (175g) lamb steaks, neck fillet or the meat in lamb chops, chopped

8oz (250g) pumpkin or squash, cubed

1 large carrot, chopped

½ tsp ground cinnamon

½ tsp ground cumin

1 tsp tomato purée

4 to 6 fresh or (400g) canned plum tomatoes

⅔ cup (150ml) water

Preheat the oven to 325°F (160°C).

Put all the ingredients in a casserole dish with a well-fitting lid. Cover and cook in the oven for 1 hour.

Remove from the oven and mash the vegetables into the gravy using a potato masher.

makes	suitable for	storage	preparation	nutritional value
3 child-sized servings	those intolerant to gluten, milk, and lactose	24 hours in the refrigerator; 1 week in the freezer	10 minutes + 1 hour cooking time	Good source of ★ iron ★ vitamin A

This recipe is suitable for younger children if you process it in a blender before serving.

Spicy Cheese and Potato Sticks

2 large (400g) mashed potato

1 cup (125g) cheddar cheese, grated

½ tsp ground coriander

1 egg yolk, beaten

a little flour for dusting

a little beaten egg or milk for brushing

1 tbsp seeds such as fennel, caraway, sesame, or sunflower, or a combination

A **GREAT SNACK** at any time of day, these potato sticks are a good way of introducing children to the complex **FLAVORS** of **SPICES**. They make a tasty alternative to store-bought snacks, which often include artificial flavorings.

Preheat the oven to 400°F (200°C).

Mix the mashed potato, cheese, coriander, and egg yolk in a bowl. Lightly flour a board or clean work surface. Roll out the potato mixture until about 1in (2.5cm) thick, then cut into finger lengths.

Brush the sticks with beaten egg or milk and roll in the seeds, gently pressing them into the potato to help them stick. Place them on a lightly oiled baking sheet and bake for 10 minutes until crispy and golden.

makes
10 sticks

suitable for
vegetarians; those intolerant to gluten

storage
24 hours
in the refrigerator

preparation
15 minutes
+ 10 minutes
cooking time

nutritional value
Good source of
★ calcium
★ iron
★ vitamin C

This is a great way to use up leftover mashed potato.

Fresh corn – from the greengrocer's, a farmer's market, or, better still, from the garden – is a true **SUPERFOOD**, rich in **NUTRIENTS** and delicious as well. Barbecued corn is fun to cook and to eat.

Barbecued Corn on the Cob

1 ear of corn per child, husk removed, cut in half

4 tbs (60g) butter, melted

Light the barbecue or preheat a gas barbecue.

Wrap each corn on the cob in foil, shiny side inwards.

Place the corn on the barbecue and cook for about 10 minutes, turning frequently with tongs.

Remove from heat, then unwrap, and drizzle with melted butter.

makes
1 per child

suitable for
vegetarians; those
intolerant to gluten

storage
eat immediately

preparation
5 minutes
+ 10 minutes
cooking time

nutritional value
Good source of
★ B vitamins
★ magnesium

Take the corn out of the foil and let it cool before giving it to young children.

Hummus

13oz (400g) canned chickpeas, rinsed and drained, or ⅔ cup (100g) dried chickpeas, soaked overnight, simmered for 60 minutes, drained

3 tbsp water

2 tbsp olive oil

freshly squeezed juice of ½ lemon

2 tsp tahini (optional)*

1 garlic clove, crushed

1 tsp chopped fresh parsley

Put the chickpeas and water in a food processor and blend until the consistency of a smooth pâté.

Add the olive oil, lemon juice, tahini, if using, and garlic and process to mix.

Transfer to a bowl and sprinkle with the parsley to serve.

* Omit the tahini if there is a history of nut allergies in the family.

Serve hummus as a **DIP** with pita bread and **VEGETABLE FINGERS** or as a sandwich or baked potato **FILLING**. It can also be served hot or cold as a **BABY FOOD PURÉE**.

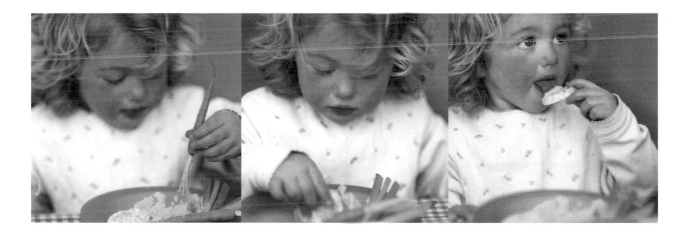

makes	suitable for	storage	preparation	nutritional value
3 child-sized servings	vegetarians; those intolerant to gluten, milk, and lactose	3 days in the refrigerator	5 minutes	Good source of ★ iron ★ vitamin C

Traditional Middle-Eastern hummus contains tahini, or sesame seed paste; add two teaspoons to boost iron levels.

This **VIBRANT**, crunchy **SALAD** is packed with nutrients that will fortify the **IMMUNE SYSTEM** and promote **GOOD DIGESTION**. Serve with baked potatoes and a protein-rich food such as dahl, **HUMMUS,** or **CREAM CHEESE**.

Energy! Energy!

1 raw beet, grated

1 apple, grated

1 carrot, grated

½ cup (60g) cabbage, finely sliced

2 tbsp (30g) sunflower seeds

small handful dried fruit such as currants or dried cranberries

2 tsp olive oil

1 tbsp freshly squeezed lemon juice, or unsweetened orange juice

1 tsp honey

Combine the grated beet, apple, carrot, and cabbage in a bowl. Mix in the sunflower seeds and dried fruit.

In a separate bowl, mix the olive oil, lemon, or orange juice and honey together until well blended. Pour the mixture over the salad and toss until the salad is evenly coated.

makes
3 child-sized portions

suitable for
vegetarians; those intolerant to gluten, milk, and lactose

storage
best eaten within 2 hours

preparation
10 minutes

nutritional value
Good source of
★ vitamin A
★ vitamin C

Use red or white cabbage and hard fruits such as pears to vary tastes and textures in this salad.

This is a **MEDITERRANEAN** take on a traditional British pudding. It uses ingredients widely used in Italian cooking such as **CITRUS** zest, olive oil, and **HERBS** and is a firm **FAVORITE** with my family.

Italian Bread and Butter Pudding

4 large slices good-quality white or whole wheat bread, buttered on one side

3 tsp (30g) raisins, currants, or cranberries, or other dried fruit such as cherries, prunes, or figs, finely chopped

½ ripe apple or pear, cored and chopped into small pieces

2 eggs

2 tbs (30g) honey

1 tsp chopped fresh or ½ tsp dried sage, rosemary, or thyme

grated zest of ½ lemon or small orange

½ tsp ground cinnamon

1¾ cups (450ml) milk

drizzle of olive oil

Preheat the oven to 350°F (180°C).

Cut the slices of bread into halves or quarters. Line the bottom of a greased ovenproof dish with one layer of bread, buttered side up. Sprinkle with a little dried fruit and apple or pear, cover with bread, and continue the layering process.

Whisk the eggs, honey, herbs, zest, cinnamon, and milk in a bowl and pour over the bread. Let stand for 30 minutes.

Drizzle over the olive oil and bake in the oven until golden, about 30 minutes.

makes
2 child-sized servings and 2 adult servings

suitable for
vegetarians

storage
24 hours in the refrigerator; 1 week in the freezer

preparation
15 minutes + 30 minutes cooking time

nutritional value
Good source of
★ calcium
★ iron

Sage, rosemary, or thyme work well in this recipe, but any dried herbs will do.

Party food doesn't have to be unhealthy – children love fresh fruit and crunchy snacks such as breadsticks.

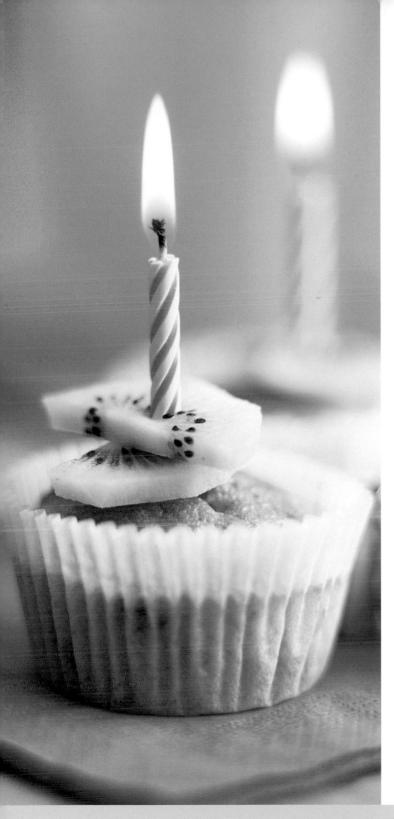

Fruity Birthday Cupcakes

6 tbs (90g) butter

2 ripe bananas, mashed

1 egg, beaten

⅓ cup (90ml) milk

1 tbsp honey

1⅔ cup (200g) self-rising flour

¼ tsp baking soda

½ cup (90g) golden raisins

1 banana, sliced, for decorating

Preheat the oven to 400°F (200°C).

Cream together the butter and banana in a bowl. Gradually work the egg, milk, honey, flour, and baking soda into the mixture. Stir in the golden raisins. Divide the mixture between small paper cake cups.

Bake for 15 minutes in the middle of the oven until a skewer inserted into the middle of a cupcake comes out clean.

Remove from the oven and cool on a cake rack. Decorate with banana slices and candles.

FOR PEAR CUPCAKES, follow the recipe above but substitute a mashed pear for one of the bananas and decorate with sliced pear pieces.

FOR STRAWBERRY CUPCAKES, follow the recipe above but substitute four mashed strawberries for one of the bananas, and decorate with sliced strawberry or kiwi pieces.

makes 24 cupcakes
suitable for vegetarians; those intolerant to milk and lactose
storage 4 days in an airtight container; 1 week in the freezer
preparation 15 minutes + 15 minutes baking time
nutritional value Good source of ★ vitamin B6 ★ vitamin C ★ magnesium ★ potassium

These festive cupcakes are made without sugar and are decorated with fresh fruit.

Pre-school

EXPLORING DIFFERENT FOODS

BETWEEN TWO AND FIVE YEARS CHILDREN BEGIN TO MOVE INTO SOCIETY, LEARNING TO BECOME MEMBERS OF MORE COMPLEX SOCIAL GROUPS.

By five years of age your child will be at school, eating meals in a range of locations, enjoying different foods, and influenced in his tastes by the people with whom he comes into contact.

As a parent, you are faced with the challenge of meeting his nutritional needs in settings you do not control. Now that many people in the US eat some organic food your child will not be unusual – an important factor, since children do not like being different. Organic bread, cheese, fruit, and drinks in a lunch box can look exactly like their conventional counterparts.

Maintaining *a* balanced diet

JUNK FOOD AND PESTER POWER

• Marketing and advertising companies often target children. They know that if they can create a desire for products, children will pester their parents for them. US children watch tens of thousands of television ads in their early years and give as much authority to ads as they do to programs in influencing their likes and dislikes.

• Advertised foods such as potato chips, candies, yogurts, drinks, and cereals are almost always highly processed, with liberal use of sugar and fat, as well as fillers and additives. They are placed on the shelf right at your child's eye level.

• You are the greatest influence over your child. If you do not feel that enough choice is available, tell the store manager or owner – they want to know and they do respond.

The importance of breakfast

Breakfast is the first meal of the day after our longest fast. When children wake up they need a quick burst of liquid, energy, and protein to give them the best start to their day. Oatmeal, bread, or rice-based cereals provide a complete package of complex carbohydrates, vitamins, minerals, and fiber that will be slowly released throughout the morning. Add to that some organic fruit juice and fresh fruit.

Eggs can provide 20 percent of the day's protein requirement and contain potassium, iodine, folic acid, vitamin C, and beta carotene. Children love French toast, omelettes, and boiled egg with toast. Free-range organic eggs are free from antibiotics, food additives, and other chemicals fed or injected into chickens. The birds are also reared in conditions that show consideration for their natural instincts.

Vegetables and citrus fruit

Until recently, eating different vegetables clearly marked the seasons, with root crops providing winter sustenance, and salads available only in the summer. When you choose organic produce you resume this way of eating because organic produce is not available in every form all year round. Nonorganic lettuce is always available because it is fed with synthetic fertilizers and repeatedly sprayed.

By four years of age your child should be eating about 2oz (60g) of vegetables each day – cooked, raw, frozen, and canned. Children usually love raw vegetables such as carrots and celery. They are

Research has shown that children who eat breakfast perform significantly better at school than those who do not.

Organic superfoods

GRAPES Packed with vitamin C, natural antioxidants, and natural sugars, grapes give your child an instant energy boost.

CITRUS FRUIT Grapefruit and oranges are rich in beta carotene, vitamin C, vitamins B1 and 6, potassium, folic acid, calcium, and iron.

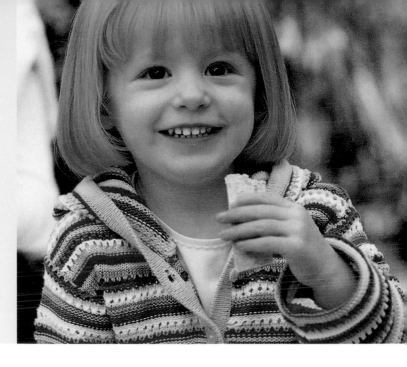

crunchy, sweet and make good finger foods – they are also extremely nutritious. Also try cucumber, which contains potassium and folic acid, as well as beta carotene in the skin. Nonorganic cucumbers should be peeled since they are waxed with a chemical wax to prolong shelf life.

Lettuce is rich in vitamins A and C, folic acid, potassium, calcium, and phosphorus. It also contains phytochemicals which naturally help to induce sleep. Organic lettuce can be obtained seasonally, and, unlike nonorganic lettuce, none of the leaves need be discarded to avoid the worst of the pesticide residues. Nonorganic produce may be sprayed with artificial pesticides, residues of which may affect the development of metabolic systems. For this reason you should always peel, tip, and tail nonorganic produce before use. This will in some cases lessen residues, but because systemic chemicals may be used, conventional vegetables may contain residues. Organic vegetables just need a quick rinse.

Children can enjoy fruit if it is fun to eat. Kiwi fruit can be eaten like a boiled egg, with a spoon, and grapes make an ideal snack. Grapefruit or oranges, as fruit or juice, are an excellent way to wake up the palate after a long sleep. In 1998, residues were found in all 50 samples of nonorganic oranges tested in the UK, so try to buy organic.

Q&A

HOW CAN I STOP MY CHILD FROM BECOMING OBESE?

Where possible, cook organic food, and keep convenience food for when you are really busy. Regard candy as a rare treat; reward with love and time instead. Don't worry if your child leaves food – let him judge when he is full.

MY CHILD SUFFERS FROM CONSTIPATION. CAN YOU RECOMMEND A LAXATIVE?

Never give laxatives to young children – they cure the symptoms but not the problem. Avoid refined foods, and include more whole foods, fruit, and vegetables in your child's diet.

Nutritious and **EASY TO PREPARE**, macaroni and **CHEESE** is popular with most children. Here is a version with added **GOURMET** ingredients for a special treat.

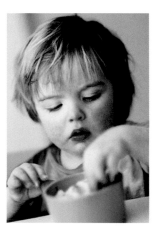

Little Gourmet Macaroni and Cheese

1¼ cup (300ml) milk

1 bay leaf

1 cup (125g) small macaroni or pasta shapes

2 tbs (30g) butter

¼ cup (30g) cornstarch or plain flour

⅓ cup (60g) hard cheese such as cheddar, grated

1 small onion, finely chopped

¾ cup (60g) button mushrooms, finely chopped

⅓ cup (60g) frozen peas

½ garlic clove, crushed

1 tsp finely chopped fresh herbs such as basil, sage, or chives

Preheat the oven to 400°F (200°C).

Heat the milk in a pan with the bay leaf. Bring to simmering point, then remove from the heat, and set aside to cool.

Cook the pasta according to the directions on the package and drain well.

In a separate pan, gently heat the butter. Add the flour and stir, using a wooden spoon or hand whisk, until well combined and smooth. Remove the bay leaf from the milk, then gradually add the milk to the pan, stirring continuously.

Stir the sauce over a medium heat until it begins to thicken. Simmer for 3 minutes, then stir in half the cheese, all the macaroni, and the onion, mushrooms, peas, garlic, and herbs.

Spoon into an ovenproof dish, sprinkle the remaining cheese over the top, and bake for 20 minutes, until the top is bubbling and golden.

makes	suitable for	storage	preparation	nutritional value
4 child-sized servings	vegetarians	24 hours in the refrigerator; 1 week in the freezer	20 minutes + 20 minutes cooking time	Good source of ★ calcium ★ vitamin C

Any fresh, green herbs will enhance the flavor of a pasta sauce – use whatever you have to hand.

SPICY food can be very **POPULAR** with children, but be careful not to overdo it – very spicy food can turn them off. Serve this with boiled **RICE** or a **FLATBREAD** such as naan or pita bread for a perfectly balanced meal.

Dahl

1 tbsp good-quality vegetable oil

1 small onion, finely chopped

½ tsp turmeric

½ tsp ground coriander or cumin seeds

½ cup (125g) red lentils, washed and picked over

1 carrot, finely chopped

1¼ cup (300ml) water

small handful shredded cabbage

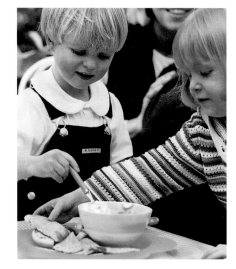

Heat the oil in a pan over medium heat. Add the onion and fry gently until soft, about 5 minutes. Mix in the spices and cook for another 2 minutes.

Add the lentils, carrot, and water and bring to a boil. Reduce the heat and simmer for 20 minutes, until the lentils are soft and the dahl has a smooth consistency. Add the cabbage and cook for another 5 minutes, stirring from time to time.

makes	suitable for	storage	preparation	nutritional value
3 child-sized servings	vegetarians; those intolerant to gluten, milk, and lactose	24 hours in the refrigerator; 1 week in the freezer	10 minutes + 25 minutes cooking time	Good source of ★ iron ★ protein

To adapt either of these recipes for adults, add crushed garlic and chopped fresh green chili to taste.

Corn Chowder

1 tsp good-quality vegetable oil or butter

2in (5cm) piece leek, well washed and sliced

¼ red pepper, finely chopped

1¼ cup (300ml) milk

⅔ cup (125g) fresh, frozen, or canned corn (unsalted, unsweetened)

1 potato, chopped

1 bay leaf

¼ cup (60ml) light cream

Heat the oil or butter in a pan over medium heat. Gently fry the leek and red pepper until soft, about 5 minutes. Add the milk, corn, potato, and bay leaf and bring to a boil.

Reduce the heat and simmer for 10 minutes or until the potato is tender. Add the cream, remove the bay leaf, and blend briefly in a food processor or blender.

A **CHOWDER** is a **THICK**, potato-based soup. This one contains **CORN** and **LEEK** and **CREAM** for added richness. Serve this with crusty bread or slices of cheese on toast.

makes
6 child-sized servings

suitable for
vegetarians; those intolerant to gluten

storage
24 hours in the refrigerator; 1 week in the freezer

preparation
15 minutes

nutritional value
Good source of
★ complex carbohydrates
★ vitamin C

Burgers are one area where **VEGETARIAN** children often feel deprived. These bean burgers can be served with baked potatoes and peas – or even covered with **TOMATO SAUCE** and served in a bun.

Spicy Bean Burgers

2 tbsp olive oil

1 onion, finely chopped

1 carrot, finely grated

1 green pepper, chopped

1 garlic clove, crushed

½ tsp ground coriander

½ tsp cumin seeds

2 x 13oz (400g) can beans such as white, flageolet, kidney, or chickpeas, rinsed and drained

1 tbsp tomato purée

1 egg, beaten

1 cup (60g) dried breadcrumbs

½ cup (60g) mature cheddar cheese, grated

salt and freshly ground black pepper

Preheat the oven to 400°F (200°C).

Heat the oil in a frying pan over medium heat. Add the onion and fry gently until soft, about 5 minutes. Add the carrot, green pepper, garlic, and spices and cook for another 5 minutes. Remove from the heat.

In a large bowl, mash the beans and tomato purée together with a fork. Mix in the onion mixture, egg, breadcrumbs, cheese, and seasoning. Divide the mixture into golf ball-sized portions and shape into burgers with your hands.

Place the burgers on an oiled baking sheet and bake in the oven until crisp, about 25 minutes. Turn the burgers half-way through cooking to crisp both sides.

makes
8 burgers

suitable for
vegetarians

storage
24 hours in the refrigerator; 1 week in the freezer

preparation
15 minutes
+ 25 minutes
cooking time

nutritional value
Good source of
★ iron

The beans and egg in these burgers are a good source of iron in the vegetarian diet.

Mild Vegetable Korma with Couscous

The **COCONUT** in this recipe mellows its **SPICINESS** and brings a delicious **CREAMINESS** to it; this is an ideal way to introduce your child to **NEW FLAVORS.**

1 tsp olive oil

1 small leek, well washed and sliced

½ tsp each ground cumin, garam masala, and turmeric

1 carrot, diced

⅓ eggplant, chopped

1 small green pepper, diced

½ cup (60g) small broccoli or cauliflower florets

¾ cup (60g) sliced mushrooms

½ cup (60g) fresh or frozen baby fava beans

1 cup (200ml) water or stock

2 tbsp tomato purée

¼ cup (60g) coconut milk

⅓ cup (125g) couscous or basmati rice

Heat the oil in a pan and fry the leek, cumin, garam masala, and turmeric for 2 minutes. Add all the other ingredients, except the coconut milk and couscous or rice and stir to mix.

Cover, bring to a boil, then reduce the heat and simmer, stirring occasionally, until the vegetables are tender, about 20 minutes.

Cook the couscous or rice according to the directions on the package.

Stir the coconut milk into the korma and heat for another 2 minutes.

Arrange the couscous or rice into a ring shape, then spoon the korma into the middle of it to serve.

makes
4 child-sized servings

suitable for
vegetarians; those intolerant to gluten, milk, and lactose

storage
24 hours in the refrigerator; 1 month in the freezer

preparation
10 minutes
+ 25 minutes cooking time

nutritional value
Good source of
★ iron
★ vitamin C

This is delicious served with naan or pita bread and natural yogurt mixed with cucumber pieces and chopped fresh mint.

Meat Burgers

1lb (500g) ground beef, lamb, or pork

1 small onion, finely chopped

½ tsp chopped fresh sage or ¼ tsp dried sage

¾ cup (60g) dried breadcrumbs

2 tsp good-quality vegetable oil, if frying the burgers

These burgers can be fried or oven cooked. If oven cooking, preheat the oven to 400°F (200°C).

Mix the meat, onion, sage, and breadcrumbs together in a bowl with your hands.

Shape the mixture into tangerine-sized balls, then flatten into burgers.

If oven cooking, place the burgers on a baking sheet and cook in the oven for about 10–15 minutes, turning them half-way through cooking. Test by inserting a skewer into the middle of a burger – there should be no trace of pink in the meat and the juices should run clear.

If frying the burgers, heat the oil in a nonstick frying pan and fry over medium heat until lightly browned, about 4 minutes on each side. Again, when a skewer is inserted into the middle of a burger, there should be no trace of pink in the meat and the juices should run clear.

Although fast food burgers are usually **TASTY**, you can't always be sure where the **INGREDIENTS** have come from. **HOMEMADE** burgers are a **TREAT** for children and are very **EASY** to prepare. Serve in a crusty or seeded bun with rings of tomato and onion and plenty of salad.

makes	suitable for	storage	preparation	nutritional value
4 large quarter-pounder or 8 standard-size burgers	those intolerant to milk and lactose	24 hours in the refrigerator	20 minutes + 10 minutes cooking time	Good source of ★ iron ★ zinc

Enlist the help of older children when preparing these burgers – they will have lots of fun and enjoy their meal even more.

As long as they are not the only food your child eats, these **CHICKEN** dippers can be a **FUN** and nutritious addition to your repertoire. Serve them with potatoes and baked beans or **RICE** with stir-fried vegetables.

Chicken Dippers and Dipping Sauces

FOR TOMATO DIPPING SAUCE:

1 large fresh tomato or (250g) canned tomatoes, chopped

½ small onion, finely chopped

1 garlic clove, crushed

2 tsp honey

1 tsp cornstarch mixed with 2 tbsp water

FOR BARBECUE DIPPING SAUCE:

Follow the recipe above, but substitute unsweetened pineapple or other tropical fruit juice for the water.

FOR CHICKEN DIPPERS:

8oz (250g) skinless, boneless chicken breast, cut into thin strips

1 tbsp cornstarch

1 cup (60g) whole wheat breadcrumbs

freshly ground black pepper

½ tsp paprika

1 small egg, beaten

a little good-quality vegetable oil, for frying

Put all the ingredients for your chosen sauce in a pan. Stir well to mix, then cover and bring to a boil. Reduce the heat and simmer, covered, for 10 minutes, stirring occasionally.

Uncover and simmer for another 15 minutes, stirring occasionally, until thickened. Blend and strain the sauce, then set aside.

Make the chicken dippers: dip the chicken strips in the cornstarch, covering them completely, and shake to remove any excess flour. Mix the breadcrumbs, pepper, and paprika together. Dip the chicken strips in the egg, then roll in the breadcrumb mixture until entirely coated.

Heat the oil in a nonstick frying pan and fry the chicken strips over a medium heat for 10–15 minutes, turning them at least once, until golden on both sides.

makes	suitable for	storage	preparation	nutritional value
10 dippers	those intolerant to milk and lactose	sauce keeps for 3 days in the refrigerator; dippers should be eaten immediately	10 minutes + 15 minutes cooking time	Good source of ★ iron

To make homemade fish sticks, substitute 2in (5cm) chunks of a firm fish such as cod, haddock, or salmon for the chicken.

This is a delicious way of serving **FRUIT** – hot and soft, it has **CRISPY BITS** but no added sugar. Serve this with **PLAIN YOGURT** and a sprinkling of **NUTS**.

Summer Baked Fruit

1 apple, cored and roughly chopped

1 pear, cored and roughly chopped

segments from 1 small orange, halved

1 nectarine or peach, pitted and roughly chopped

1 banana, sliced

2 tbsp unsweetened orange or grapefruit juice

½ tsp cinnamon

Preheat the oven to 350°F (180°C).

Place all the fruit in a shallow ovenproof dish. Add the orange or grapefruit juice and toss to coat the fruit. Sprinkle the cinnamon over the top.

Cover the dish with foil and bake in the oven, stirring occasionally, until the fruit is soft, about 20 minutes.

Remove the foil and crisp the surface of the fruit by baking for another 15 minutes.

makes	suitable for	storage	preparation	nutritional value
3 child-sized servings	vegetarians; those intolerant to gluten, milk, and lactose	24 hours in the refrigerator	10 minutes + 35 minutes cooking time	Good source of ★ vitamin C

This makes a light, delicate summer dessert, but would also make a wonderful breakfast treat served cold.

Whole wheat Pancakes

3⅔ cups (900ml) milk or buttermilk

3 eggs, beaten

¼ cup (60g) good-quality vegetable oil or melted butter

1½ cups (175g) plain white flour

1⅔ cups (175g) whole wheat flour

1 tsp cinnamon

⅔ cup (125g) raisins, dried cranberries, or sour cherries

a little good-quality vegetable oil, for frying

Beat together the milk or buttermilk, eggs, and oil or butter. Add the flour and cinnamon and beat until the batter is smooth, then let stand for 30 minutes. Stir in the dried fruit.

Heat a lightly oiled nonstick frying pan and pour in a small ladleful, about 3 tablespoons, of batter. Cook over medium heat until lightly browned, about 2–3 minutes on each side.

Children love these nutritious pancakes **ROLLED** up, **FOLDED,** or eaten **FLAT.** They are great served with bananas, kiwis, or peaches and cream cheese, or **HONEY** and **YOGURT.**

makes	suitable for	storage	preparation	nutritional value
15–20 pancakes	vegetarians	best eaten immediately	45 minutes + 20 minutes cooking time	Good source of ★ calcium ★ iron

Try making something different for a weekend **BREAKFAST** or a **SNACK-TIME TREAT**. These **MOIST** muffins have a **DISTINCTIVE TASTE** and **SMELL** that children love.

Raisin Bran Muffins

3 cups (300g) unsweetened organic bran cereal

2¾ cups (300g) whole wheat flour

2 tsp baking powder

2 large eggs, beaten

½ cup (125ml) good-quality vegetable oil

½ cup (125ml) molasses or (60m) honey and ¼ cup (60ml) molasses

1¼ cups (300ml) milk

⅔ cup (125g) raisins or golden raisins

Preheat the oven to 350°F (180°C.

Combine the cereal, flour, and baking powder in a large bowl.

In a separate bowl, blend the eggs, oil, and molasses, or honey, milk, and raisins.

Mix all the ingredients together, stirring just until mixed.

Spoon the mixture into greased muffin pans, making sure not to fill them more than two-thirds full. Bake until golden and starting to come away from the sides of the pan, about 25–30 minutes.

makes	suitable for	storage	preparation	nutritional value
12 muffins	vegetarians	4 days in an airtight container	10 minutes + 25–30 minutes cooking time	Good source of ★ calcium ★ magnesium ★ potassium

Muffin pans are usually available from kitchen stores; if you can't find them, use paper cupcake shells and bake for just 15 minutes.

The idea is **SIMPLE** – take the most **DELICIOUS FRUITS** you can find, just **RIPE** and ready to eat, and blend them with **CRUSHED ICE** for **SMOOTHIES** or **MILK** for **MILKSHAKES**.

Fresh and Fruity Shakes

1¼ cups (300ml) milk*, or freshly squeezed juice of 2 oranges

½ glass crushed ice (ice cubes crushed with a rolling pin)

FOR BANANA SHAKE:
add 1 sliced banana

FOR PEAR SHAKE:
add 1 cored and chopped pear

FOR BERRY SHAKE:
add 1 handful strawberries, raspberries, blackberries, or blueberries, or a combination

FOR PEACH SHAKE:
add 1 pitted and chopped ripe peach or nectarine

*rice, soy, and follow-up milks may be substituted

Put the milk or orange juice and crushed ice in a blender. Add the fruit of your choice.

Blend the mixture at high speed until smooth, thick, and bubbly.

Pour into glasses and serve immediately.

makes	suitable for	storage	preparation	nutritional value
1 serving	vegetarians; those intolerant to gluten	best drunk immediately	5 minutes	Good source of ★ vitamin C

These healthy shakes are full of nutrients and are an ideal way to encourage your child to enjoy fresh fruit.

Meal
planners

4–7 months

Every baby is different. Be guided by your baby's interest in the food and his appetite. Start with single flavor purées, then try him with the more varied recipes suggested for this age group. Once your baby can take food from a spoon, offer second and third meals at two-weekly intervals.

	BREAKFAST	MID A.M.	LUNCH	MID P.M.	DINNER	BEDTIME
from weaning	Breast milk or formula milk	Breast milk or formula milk	Breast milk or formula milk	Breast milk or formula milk	3 tsp baby rice mixed with breast or formula milk	Breast milk or formula milk
after 2 weeks	3 tsp baby rice mixed with breast or formula milk	Breast milk or formula milk	Breast milk or formula milk	Breast milk or formula milk	2 tbsp puréed apple	Breast milk or formula milk
after 4 weeks menu 1	2 tbsp baby rice mixed with breast or formula milk	Breast milk or formula milk	Baby's First Vegetables*	Breast milk or formula milk	Fruit Compote*	Breast milk or formula milk
menu 2	Apple and Apricot Purée*	Breast milk or formula milk	Potato, carrot, and broccoli purée	Breast milk or formula milk	Banana and Berries*	Breast milk or formula milk

*recipe included in book, see Index

7–10 months

During this stage your baby will be enjoying three meals a day and will have tried a range of foods. Now offer breast or formula milk after food, rather than before it, especially at breakfast time – milk will take the edge off your baby's appetite if given before solid food. You should now introduce iron-rich foods such as meat, fish, legumes, and leafy green vegetables. These foods provide your baby with iron and protein as well as a range of minerals and vitamins needed to aid growth.

	BREAKFAST	MID A.M.	LUNCH	MID P.M.	DINNER	BEDTIME
menu 1	Prune and Apple Hot Cereal*	Breast milk or formula milk	Pasta with Tomato and Cheese Sauce *	Breast milk or formula milk	Fruity Rice with Chicken and Apricot* *or* Baby's First Vegetables*	Breast milk or formula milk
menu 2	Apple and Banana Breakfast*	Breast milk or formula milk	Corn and Potato*	Breast milk or formula milk	Tomato and Chicken Casserole* *or* Potato and Cheese Dinner*	Breast milk or formula milk
menu 3	Banana and Fig Hot Cereal*	Breast milk or formula milk	Vegetable and Coconut Korma*	Breast milk or formula milk	Pasta with Bolognese Sauce* or Broccoli gratin	Breast milk or formula milk
menu 4	Banana and Mango Coulis*	Breast milk or formula milk	Mediterranean Vegetables and Chicken*	Breast milk or formula milk	Pasta with Tomato and Basil Sauce	Breast milk or formula milk
menu 5	Apricot Hot Cereal*	Breast milk or formula milk	Poached fish and potato and broccoli purée	Breast milk or formula milk	Cauliflower and cheese	Breast milk or formula milk

*recipe included in book, see Index

10–15 months

Your baby will now have a well-established mealtime pattern. Babies are happiest when secure in a routine. This is the age to eat food with the family – your baby may enjoy sharing your meal with you, and much of the food he eats will be suitable for the whole family. He will need about about 2 cups of milk by now, including milk used in cooking and in milk products such as cheese and yogurt.

	BREAKFAST	LUNCH	DINNER
menu 1	Breakfast Surprise*	Pasta with Creamy Mushroom Sauce*	Mini Meatballs in Herby Tomato Sauce* or Corn and Potato* Baked Bananas*
menu 2	Mixed Fruit Compote*	Pumpkin Stew-in-a-Pot* or Pasta with Tomato and Basil Sauce*	Baked Potato with Avocado Dip* Rice Pudding with Apricots*
menu 3	Apricot Hot Cereal*	Fish Cakes* or Vegetable and Coconut Korma*	Tomato and Chicken Casserole* or Corn and Potato* Banana and Mango Coulis*
menu 4	Scrambled Egg with Whole wheat Toast	Beef Casserole* or Days Out Cakes* with mashed boiled egg	Baked Potato with Dahl* Berries and Cherries*
menu 5	Apple and Banana Breakfast*	Dahl with rice*	Fish Cakes* or Pasta with Tomato and Cheese Sauce* Fresh fruit

*recipe included in book, see Index

Toddler

Toddlers like to graze and snack, and they need the frequent bursts of energy provided by snacks to fuel their growth and development. A slice of organic bread is more nutritious than a cookie, and a banana is a more suitable energy-rich food than a package of potato chips. Water is the best drink, but for variety, you could try fresh organic fruit juice diluted with water (one part juice to two parts water).

	BREAKFAST	LUNCH	DINNER
menu 1	Apple and Orange Breakfast*	Roasted Lima Bean Gratin*	Mediterranean Lamb* *or* Fish Cakes* Mixed Fruit Compote*
menu 2	Baked beans and mushrooms on whole wheat toast	Baked Potato with chicken, red and green peppers, and butter* *or* with Hummus*	Sausages with Mashed Potatoes * *or* Pasta with Tomato and Basil Sauce* Italian Bread and Butter Pudding*
menu 3	Banana and grapefruit segments Toast with butter	Pumpkin Stew in-a-Pot* *or* Pasta with Creamy Mushroom Sauce*	Beef Casserole* *or* Vegetable and Coconut Korma* Fruit Bread Fingers,* yogurt, and chopped strawberries
menu 4	Boiled egg with rye toast	Avocado Dip* with pitta bread and Energy! Energy!* or other salad	Fruity Rice with Chicken and Apricot* (not puréed) with Barbecue Corn on the Cob* Berries and Cherries*
menu 5	Hot Cereal with chopped fruit	Baked Potato with brussels sprouts, tuna fish, and a little olive oil*	Dahl with pita bread* Fresh fruit salad

*recipe included in book, see Index

Pre-school

This is the age of conformity. Children want to be like their peers, but also want to be part of the family. It is good to share one meal a day, even if it is simply an after-school snack (see opposite).

You can continue to influence your child's eating habits by keeping nutritious healthy food in the cupboard and fridge and making meals a time of relaxation and pleasure.

	BREAKFAST	LUNCH	DINNER
menu 1	Bacon with tomato and mushrooms and whole wheat toast	Little Gourmet Macaroni and Cheese* with Energy! Energy!* or other salad	Sausages with Mashed Potato and Gravy * *or* Baked Potato with Dahl* Summer Baked Fruit*
menu 2	Apple and Orange Breakfast* Toast	Corn Chowder* with Cheese on toast	Chicken Dippers and Dipping Sauces* *or* Fish Cakes* with mixed salad Whole wheat Pancakes*
menu 3	Whole wheat cereal and plain live yogurt with banana and tangerine	Meat Burgers* *or* Spicy Bean Burgers* with home-made coleslaw	Mild Vegetable Korma with Couscous* Rice Pudding with Apricots*
menu 4	Boiled egg with whole wheat toast	Baked sweet potato with onion, mushroom, zucchini, and goat's cheese*	Mini Meatballs in Herby Tomato Sauce* *or* Pasta with Creamy Mushroom Sauce* Mixed Fruit Compote*
menu 5	Whole wheat Pancakes*	Fish Cakes* *or* Dahl with rice*	Pasta with Tomato and Basil Sauce* Raisin Bran Muffin*

*recipe included in book, see Index

Food for all occasions

quick fixes

Asterisked recipes take 15 minutes or less; others take 20 minutes or less.

It takes no time at all to prepare healthy and delicious food that your child will enjoy. The secret is a well-stocked pantry.

4–7 months:
- Apple and Apricot Purée
- Fruit Compote
- Banana and Berries*
- Fruity Hot Cereals* (Banana , Prune, and Apple or Apricot Hot Cereal)

7–10 months:
- Apple and Banana breakfast
- Banana and Fig Hot Cereal*
- Rice Pudding with Apricots*

10–15 months:
- Mixed Fruit Compote*
- Pasta with Creamy Mushroom Sauce*
- Avocado Dip*
- Scrambled or boiled eggs with toast*
- Baked beans on whole wheat toast*

Toddler:
- Apple and Orange Breakfast*
- Sausages with Mashed Potatoes and Gravy*
- Hummus*
- Energy! Energy!*

Pre-school:
- Corn Chowder*
- Fresh and Fruity Shakes*

snacks

Avoid highly processed snack foods, which are high in sugar, fat, and salt. There are plenty of tasty and nutritious alternatives.

- Fresh fruit such as apples, banana, grapes, kiwis, mangoes, nectarines, peaches, pears, berries, and tangerines cut into manageable pieces or chopped and served with yogurt
- Dried fruit
- Juices
- Rice crackers (unsalted varieties)
- Whole wheat toast with butter or cheese
- Alfalfa sprouts, chickpeas, lentils, mung beans, etc.
- Mini rice cakes, pita bread, and breadsticks
- Cherry tomatoes and vegetable sticks such as carrots, celery, and cucumber served with dips such as hummus, avocado dip, or yogurt with chopped cucumber and mint

family meals

Remember to remove your child's portion before adding salt or hot spices. Be aware of the need for different textures at different ages.

- Mediterranean Vegetables and Chicken
- Pasta with Tomato and Basil Sauce
- Pasta with Bolognese Sauce
- Pasta with Tomato and Cheese Sauce
- Vegetable and Coconut Korma
- Fruity Rice with Chicken and Apricot
- Rice Pudding with Apricots
- Fish Cakes
- Beef Casserole
- Mini Meatballs in Herby Tomato Sauce
- Pumpkin Stew-in-a Pot
- Baked Bananas
- Roasted Lima Bean Gratin
- Sausages with Mashed Potatoes
- Mediterranean Lamb
- Barbecue Corn on the Cob
- Italian Bread and Butter Pudding
- Little Gourmet Macaroni & Cheese
- Dahl
- Spicy Bean Burgers
- Mild Vegetable Korma with Couscous
- Meat Burgers
- Summer Baked Fruit

party food

This is food that children can have fun with. Your child might like to help you decorate cakes or muffins with fresh fruit.

- Days Out Cakes
- Fruit Bread Fingers
- Spicy Cheese and Potato Sticks
- Raisin Bran Muffins
- Fresh and Fruity Shakes
- Fruity Birthday Cupcakes

HEALTH
ISSUES
and NUTRITION

During pregnancy or while breast-feeding

it is particularly important to eat a healthy,

balanced diet as the nutrients that you eat

are passed on to your baby. Raising your

child on a vegetarian or vegan diet requires

careful planning, and you may also need to

adapt your child's diet to deal with digestive

or allergic problems.

Pregnancy *and* breast-feeding

DIET ESSENTIALS DURING PREGNANCY

Your baby eats what you eat. Consider the following guidelines for a healthy, balanced diet:

• Make fresh organic bread, pasta, legumess, potatoes, and rice the foundation foods; they provide lots of energy as well as protein, vitamins, and minerals

• Eat at least five servings of fresh fruit and vegetables a day

• Eat 2oz (60g) – 3½oz (100g) of protein a day; meat, fish, cheese, eggs, and legumes are good sources

• Monitor fat intake: fat should constitute about 35% of your diet, with no more than 10% coming from animal sources; use olive oil for cooking and in dressings; eat oily fish twice a week to provide the Omega 3 oil important for building your baby's brain, eyes, and nerves

• Include good sources of iron in your diet such as meat, fish, legumes, leafy green vegetables, and wholegrains; half of your iron is absorbed by your baby.

A diet for optimum health

In the 1950s and 1960s, Dr. Ancel Keys and colleagues studied the effects of diet on the health of over 12,000 men from around the world, including Greece, Italy, Croatia, Serbia, Japan, Finland, the Netherlands, and the US. The results showed that there was less heart disease in Mediterranean countries, and this is thought to be linked to their healthier diet. For instance, Mediterranean men eat less animal fat and far more complex carbohydrates such as pasta, bread, and beans, than do men in northern Europe. The oil they eat is derived from olive oil or oily fish, and they eat large quantities of fresh fruit and vegetables, especially tomatoes.

As the same quality and variety of foods are readily available in the US, anyone can adopt a similar pattern of eating, and this will meet all nutritional needs during pregnancy and while breast-feeding.

Why organic is important to the fetus

During pregnancy, good nutrition is doubly important because two people are reliant on one person's diet. Babies need to absorb not only all the nutrients they need from their mother's bloodstream, via the placenta, but also antibodies, which protect them from disease.

There is evidence that harmful substances can cross the placental barrier and affect the fetus. Even cigarette manufacturers now acknowledge the damage that tobacco can cause, and prospective parents are advised to stop smoking and to avoid smoky atmospheres. Alcohol can also be harmful in high doses. It can cause fetal alcohol syndrome, which produces abnormal physical and mental development.

It is reasonable to assume that the undesirable elements in conventional foods will be passed on to the growing embryo. As babies are at greater risk from pesticide residues, additives, and toxins than are adults, it makes sense to avoid pesticides while you are pregnant.

The early weeks of pregnancy are a critical time as the baby's vital organs and limbs are forming. You can give your child the best possible start by eating plenty of wholesome, organic food.

Nutritional advice for expectant mothers

Because a pregnant woman's body ensures that her baby gets the nutrients it needs first, it is important to eat good, organic wholefoods that maintain your own health and vitality. Make sure that your diet is rich in minerals such as iron and calcium to prevent conditions such as anemia and pregnancy-related osteoporosis. Calcium is best absorbed from natural sources (green vegetables, whole wheat bread, beans, and lentils) rather than supplements because excesses cannot be stored in the body. Vitamin D is essential since it helps the body to absorb calcium.

Folic acid deficiency needs to be avoided as this has been linked to spina bifida in babies. Supplements are recommended three months prior to conception and in the first three months of pregnancy, but you can also obtain folic acid from your diet. Many foods rich in folic acid are also rich in other essential nutrients. They include brussels sprouts, spinach, cauliflower, broccoli, cabbage, lettuce, green beans, peas, carrots, tomatoes, oranges, grapefruit, brown rice, potatoes, and meat products. Be wary of breakfast cereals that are fortified with folic acid – they may be highly processed and high in sugar.

It is best to avoid raw eggs because of the risk of being infected with salmonella, and also pâté and soft cheese because of the risk of listeria. Try to eat a healthier diet and cut down on processed foods, as they are usually rich in cheap ingredients that are high in additives, sugar, fats, and salt. Finally, reduce your caffeine intake and avoid artificial sweeteners – try to change your long-term diet to improve your own health as well as that of your baby.

A HEALTHY DIET DURING BREAST-FEEDING

What you eat can be passed on to your baby through your milk. If your diet lacks nutrients such as essential fats and zinc, your milk may lack these nutrients too. Follow these guidelines:

• Try to eat a good, balanced wholefood diet that includes plenty of fresh fruit, vegetables, and fiber-rich foods

• Avoid stimulants such as alcohol and caffeine

• Avoid hot, spicy foods

• Drink at least 2 litres of fluids a day to replace the breast milk lost

• Tell your pharmacist or doctor that you are breast-feeding before they suggest any medicines for you.

The key to successful breast-feeding is plenty of rest and a varied diet of small, frequent meals.

the Vegetarian baby and child

PROTEINS FOR VEGANS AND VEGETARIANS

Proteins are made from amino acids and are important body builders, necessary for maintaining tissue and sustaining growth. The body manufactures much of the protein we need itself, the rest we get from food. Plant sources of protein can meet the body's needs just as well as animal sources. While vegetarians get protein from dairy products and eggs, vegans can derive it from the following sources:

• Nuts such as peanuts, almonds, brazil nuts, and hazelnuts (see Essential Nutrients, opposite)

• Seeds such as pumpkin, sunflower, and sesame

• Legumes and beans such as soy, lentils, chickpeas, and kidney beans

• Wholegrains found in foods such as whole wheat bread and pasta, oats, and wholegrain rice.

Ensuring a nutritionally balanced diet

It is estimated that three percent of children in the UK, for example, follow a vegetarian or vegan diet. There are three types of vegetarian: those who exclude meat, poultry, and fish from their diet; others who also exclude eggs; and vegans, who additionally exclude dairy products.

All of these choices mean that you must take more responsibility for ensuring that the diet is nutritionally balanced. Eating enough of the right nutrients in a meat-based diet is a relatively easy thing to do in most cultures because there is a wide choice of foods. But when you exclude foods from your diet, you need to know what impact this can have on your long-term health. Nowhere is this more important than in planning your child's diet – childhood is such a critical period of body building that it has an impact on your child's health for the rest of his life. Vegetarianism does not need to be associated with a reduction in choice – it often means a healthier and more varied diet. But it does need more care in its construction to ensure that it is life-enhancing.

Veganism

Of particular concern is veganism, because without careful planning it can be difficult to provide the nutrients essential for a growing child. You should breast-feed for at least the first year of your baby's life and take vitamin supplements, especially vitamin B12, which can be deficient in the vegan diet. If you choose to give your baby formula milk, there are soy-based varieties available, and you should feed your baby this for two years. Because soy formula milk is high in sugars, cup-feeding from six months is recommended to protect children's teeth, and you should try to have your baby drinking from a cup by the age of one. By this age, offer milk at mealtimes only, and never before going to bed. Seek advice from a health professional before feeding soy-based baby formula to your baby.

Why organic food is so important

Vegans and vegetarians will especially benefit from organic fruits and vegetables because produce reaches the customer more quickly after harvesting, and therefore the nutrient content is likely to be higher than in nonorganic produce. This is particularly the case with the less stable, water-soluble vitamins such as vitamin C. Research is beginning to demonstrate that because organic produce grows in accordance with its natural growth cycle, nourished by rich topsoil and not forced with artificial fertilizers and growth regulators, the mature fruit or vegetable is likely to have more solid matter rich in nutrients. Additionally, organic fruit and vegetables are not waxed to prolong their shelf life, which means that there is less time for their nutrients to deteriorate.

Essential nutrients

Where possible, use whole versions of foods, for example wholegrain rice, as the nutrient content of these foods is likely to be higher than their refined counterparts. Vegetarian and vegan pantries can contain true convenience foods such as beans, legumes, and whole grains. Cheese, dairy products, and eggs are great energy foods for vegetarian babies. Vegans need to replace the nutrient-dense energy foods such as meat and eggs with a range of nuts and seeds and their oils and butters. Almond butter and tahini (sesame spread) are popular choices. However, some of these foods are known allergens (see pages 136–37) and there is controversy as to when they should be given to children. If there is a history of allergies in the family, whether it is asthma, eczema, or a food allergy, discuss the weaning needs of your vegetarian or vegan baby with a health professional before you begin.

NUTRIENT DEFICIENCY RISKS

Bear the following nutrient deficiency risks in mind when planning meals for your vegetarian or vegan child:

• Iron and zinc: good sources are whole wheat bread, rice, oats, nuts, legumes, tofu, soy protein, miso, parsley, and bean sprouts

• Vitamin B12: yeast extract, margarines, and breakfast cereals are good sources

• Vitamin D: the best source is dairy products or the action of sunlight on the skin; vegans may need to take supplements

• Vitamin B2: mushrooms, fortified breakfast cereals, and yeast extract are good sources

• Vitamin A: carrots, spinach, pumpkins, tomatoes, dark green vegetables, and vegan margarine are good sources.

Parents can now choose from a range of 100% organic baby foods, many of which are vegetarian or vegan.

Special diets *for* your child

HYPERACTIVITY

Children who are hyperactive have unusually short attention spans and are often excitable and impetuous. Hyperactivity may be the result of:

• Disruption of the brain chemistry

• Eating too many foods processed with refined carbohydrates and loaded with additives.

If you suspect that your child's hyperactivity may be related to diet, seek advice from a health professional who may advise taking the following steps:

• Replace any suspect foods with organic wholefood alternatives

• Keep a record of your child's diet and behavior.

If this does not solve the problem, talk to your health professional again. He or she is trained to help with your child's behavior and can refer you to experts who can provide you with support.

Common food allergies

Much has been written about food allergies, some of it alarmist and much of it contradictory. Words such as food intolerance, adverse reaction, and hypersensitivity add to the mystery. Put simply, an allergy is where the body reacts to a harmless substance, such as a food, as if it was harmful. This can be very serious.

The allergic reaction

A baby can develop a reaction to a food in the uterus, via breast milk, or when he first eats the food. In an allergy, his body produces antibodies called immunoglobulins on first contact with the allergen (the food). When the food and antibodies meet again this triggers the allergic reaction, which can take the form of asthma, eczema, mouth or tongue swelling, hayfever, rash, diarrhea, or abdominal pain.

Reducing the risk

If your baby experiences this type of reaction, the allergen must be identified and excluded, as further contact could produce more intense reactions. A family history of allergies may double your child's risk of allergy, so seek a pediatric dietician's advice if this is the case. Breast-feeding for at least four to six months will provide your baby with protective antibodies. Foods known to be allergens should not be given until after six months of age. Conventional processed foods, which contain a plethora of additives, as well as possible artificial chemical and antibiotic residues, place extra pressure on the immune systems of sensitive babies. This can be avoided by opting for organic alternatives.

Common allergens

Foods commonly associated with allergies are cow's milk, eggs, nuts, wheat, strawberries, citrus fruits, fish, shellfish, and sesame seeds. However, it is important that your child eats a wide variety of wholesome foods. Do not exclude foods on suspicion of allergy without talking to your doctor, because a restrictive diet can result in malnutrition.

Peanuts, and ingredients derived from them, are widely used in food processing which may be why this allergy is appearing more often. It is advised that children should avoid peanuts before five years of age. Always read the labels to check that foods are nut-free.

Digestive problems

Diarrhea, constipation, colic, and spitting up are common digestive problems that can cause much anxiety.

Gastroenteritis, a bowel inflammation caused by infection, is the most common cause of diarrhea and can be very serious in infants. It is important to get medical help since infants dehydrate quickly and lose essential nutrients. Diarrhea can be a side effect of drugs, especially antibiotics, or it may be diet-related and indicate a lactose or gluten intolerance or even too much fiber or fruit juice in the diet. In these cases changes to the diet, where advised, will be effective.

Constipation can be painful and distressing. In bottle-fed babies it may be a sign that the milk is too concentrated. When the problem occurs in children who eat mainly processed foods, it can be resolved by adding whole wheat bread, fruit, and vegetables to the diet.

Babies with colic draw up their legs in pain after a feeding and cry loudly, sometimes for hours. Gentle rocking movements, such as pushing your baby in a carriage may help, and baby massage can be effective.

Most babies spit up, or regurgitate, small amounts of food after meals. Holding your baby still in a upright position after feeding may help, so might taking your baby's weight on one hand while gently massaging his back as this allows food to settle.

WEIGHT PROBLEMS IN BABIES

By the end of their first year, most babies will have tripled their birth weight. The following weight problems are generally quite rare in babies:

- **Obesity**

In the past, plump babies developed into muscular toddlers as they became more active. Today increasing numbers become obese. They eat more sugary, processed foods than ever before and are also more sedentary, preferring to watch television rather than play outside.

- **Underweight babies**

Some babies do not grow at a steady pace. There are organizations that can advise suitable foods and quantities for underweight babies or you can visit your pediatrician.

Introduce your baby to new foods one at a time so that the cause of any allergic reaction will be more obvious.

Seasonal produce guide

Choosing to eat seasonally should mean that you eat the freshest fruit and vegetables available as well as supporting your local rural economy. This chart will give you an idea of what produce is available each season.

Fruits

	Spring Early	Spring Mid	Spring Late	Summer Early	Summer Mid	Summer Late	Autumn Early	Autumn Mid	Autumn Late	Winter Early	Winter Mid	Winter Late
Apples: Macintosh								•	•	•	•	•
Macoun								•	•	•	•	•
Empire				•	•	•	•	•	•	•	•	•
Gala							•	•	•	•	•	•
Blackberries				•	•	•	•	•				
Cherries				•	•							
Pears: Comice	•	•						•	•	•	•	•
Bosc	•							•	•	•	•	•
Plums				•	•	•	•	•				
Raspberries				•	•	•	•	•	•			
Strawberries				•	•	•	•	•	•			

Herbs

	Spring Early	Spring Mid	Spring Late	Summer Early	Summer Mid	Summer Late	Autumn Early	Autumn Mid	Autumn Late	Winter Early	Winter Mid	Winter Late
Basil		•	•	•	•	•	•	•				
Chives		•	•	•	•	•	•	•	•	•		
Mint		•	•	•	•	•	•	•	•			
Parsley		•	•	•	•	•	•	•	•			
Rosemary	•	•	•	•	•	•	•	•	•	•		
Sage		•	•	•	•	•	•	•	•			

Vegetables

Vegetables	Spring Early	Spring Mid	Spring Late	Summer Early	Summer Mid	Summer Late	Autumn Early	Autumn Mid	Autumn Late	Winter Early	Winter Mid	Winter Late
Eggplant			●	●	●	●	●					
Beans: Fava				●	●							
Runner					●	●	●	●				
Brussels sprouts	●						●	●	●	●	●	●
Cabbage: Red	●	●	●	●	●	●	●	●	●	●	●	●
Spring greens	●	●	●							●	●	●
Savoy	●	●	●		●		●		●	●	●	●
White	●	●	●	●	●	●	●	●	●	●	●	●
Broccoli			●	●	●	●	●	●	●			
Carrots				●	●	●	●	●	●	●		
Cauliflowers			●	●	●	●	●	●	●	●		
Celery				●	●	●	●	●				
Zucchini			●	●	●	●	●					
Cucumbers		●	●	●	●	●	●	●	●	●		
Leeks	●						●	●	●	●	●	●
Lettuce			●	●	●	●	●	●	●			
Snowpeas				●	●	●	●	●				
Summer squash			●	●	●	●	●					
Parsnips	●						●	●	●	●	●	●
Peas			●	●	●	●	●	●				
Potatoes: Maincrop						●	●	●	●	●		
New			●	●								
Pumpkins					●	●	●	●	●	●	●	●
Purple sprouting broccoli		●	●									
Spinach				●	●	●	●	●				
Scallions			●	●	●	●						
Rutabaga					●	●	●	●	●	●	●	●
Sweet peppers				●	●	●	●					
Tomatoes			●	●	●	●	●					
Turnips					●	●	●	●	●	●	●	●
Watercress	●	●	●	●	●	●	●	●	●			

Visiting a farmer's market is a great way to learn when local fruits and vegetables are in season.

Useful
addresses

environmental groups

FRIENDS OF THE EARTH (FOE)

1025 Vermont Ave NW

Washington,DC 20005-6

phone: 202-783-7400,

877-843-8687

f: 202-783-0444

www.foe.org/safefood

GREENPEACE USA

564 Mission Street PO Box 416

San Francisco, CA 94105

1-800-326-0959

www.greenpeaceusa.org/ge/

MOTHERS AND OTHERS FOR A LIVABLE PLANET

40 West 20th Stret

NY NY 10011-4211

212 242-0010

www.igc.apc.org/mothers

NATIONAL GEOGRAPHIC SOCIETY

1145 17th Street N.W.

Washington, D.C. 20036-4688

P.O. Box 98199

Washington, D.C. 20090-8199

www.nationalgeographic.com

THE SIERRA CLUB

85 Second St.

San Francisco, CA 94105-3441.

www.sierraclub.org

food safety

CAMPAIGN TO LABEL GENETICALLY ENGINEERED FOODS

PO Box 55699

Seattle, WA 98155

425-771-4049

www.thecampaign.org

CENTER FOR FOOD SAFETY

66 Pensylvania Ave SE Suite 302

Washington, DC 20003

202-547-9359

www.centerforfoodsafety.org

MOTHERS FOR NATURAL LAW

PO Box 1900

Fairfield, IA 52556

515-472-2040

www.safe-food.org.

health matters

CITIZENS FOR HEALTH

800-357-2211

www.citizens.org

LA LECHE LEAGUE INTERNATIONAL

PO Box 1209

Franklin Park, IL 60131

800-LA-LECHE

www.lalecheleague.org

MOTHERS AND OTHERS FOR A LIVABLE PLANET

40 West 20th Stret

NY NY 10011-4211

212 242-0010

www.igc.apc.org/mothers

MOTHERS FOR NATURAL LAW

PO Box 1900

Fairfield, IA 52556

515-472-2040

www.safe-food.org

PEOPLE'S EARTH NETWORK

2192 Massachusetts Ave

Cambridge, MA 02140

617-491-7646

www.peoplesearth.org

UNION OF CONCERNED SCIENTISTS

2 Brattle Square

Cambridge, MA 02238-9105

617-547-5552

www.ucsusa.org

organic food suppliers

EBERLY POULTRY FARMS

1095 Mount Airy Road

Stevens, PA 17578

717-336-6905

www.eberlypoultry.com

GOODNESS GREENESS

5959 South Lowe

Chicago, IL 60621

773-224-4411

www.goodnessgreeness.com

ORGANIC VALLEY FAMILY OF FARMS
CROPP COOPERATIVE

507 W. Main Street

La Farge, WI 54639

888-444-6455

ww.organicvalley.com

SHELBURNE FARMS

Shelburne, VT 05482

802-985-8686

WOLFE'S NECK FARM

10 Burnett Road

Freeport, ME 04032

Index

Figures in **bold** indicate recipes.

Acknowledgments

AUTHOR'S APPRECIATION

Many people have made this book possible: Mike Thrasher, Zoe Letts, Kim Teal, Marie Van Hagen, and especially Mary Daly and Jackie Gray at Organix all contributed ideas, time, and hard work to the researching and writing of it – even over Christmas!
Professor John Wargo of the Department of Environmental Sciences at Yale University; Dr Vyvyan Howard, Pediatric Toxicologist at the University of Liverpool; Dr Michael Crawford at the Institute of Brain Chemistry; Betsy Lydon at Mothers & Others, New York; Patrick Holden, Policy Director at the Soil Association; Tim Lobstein and Sue Dibb of the Food Commission; Joanna Blythman; Suzannah Olivier; Michael Van Straten, and health visitors nationwide have all inspired key sections of the book. The work they do on behalf of children's health inspires and motivates all of us at Organix every day.
Thanks to my mother and father, Richard and Betty Vann, for sharing their determination to achieve goals and their love of good food at an early age; Lynda Brown for her good ideas and Derek Cooper and Nigel Slater for talking and writing about good food in such a mouthwatering way – an inspiration to us all!

And finally, thanks to everyone at Dorling Kindersley for making this book what it is. Especially to Nasim Mawji, my editor, for her enormous patience and persistence when nothing seemed to be happening and to Simon Brown and the design team for making this book so attractive. And, of course, to Rosemary Scuolar at PFD for making it happen!

Dorling Kindersley would like to thank the National Farmers' Union for the Seasonal Produce Guide; Liz Bauwens for styling; Angela Haldane for photographic assistance; Valerie Lewis Chandler for the index. Thanks to the following for kindly loaning equipment and props: Bombay Duck, London; The Conran Shop, London; Eccentrics (mail order); Geoffrey Drayton, London; Urchin (mail order). Thanks to our models: Jamie Banghard, Joseph Belcher, Finn Brown, Georgina Caine, Alex Calver, Amirah Chiori, Luisa Cross, Emily Davis, Ardan Devine, Chen Dew, Myfanwy Dew, Christian El-Shamma, Star Epiphany, Paschal Golding, Tariq Jogee, Robert King, Finlay Mackenzie, Lily Marr-Johnson, Lily McCarthy, Jasper Morley, Max Napier, Eloise Newton, Morgan Oxley-King, Max Ridley, Ruby Ridley, Cheiko Sato, Natalie Shepherd, George Stephenson, Tomos Vaughan-Streater, Jasper Watt, Kathryn Watt, and Kate Wilson.